Poor Relief
in
Merthyr Tydfil Union
in
Victorian Times

Workhouse It was proposed by H. A. Bruce Esqre Seconded by D W James Esqre to be erected   That the interests of humanity and economy would be equally promoted by the erection of a workhouse.

Moved by Mr William Rees Seconded by Mr William Richards That the question be not entertained for the present: when there appeared

For the ammendment

Mr William Rees
  ,, John Williams
  ,, Griffith Davis
  ,, Richard Evans
  ,, David Davis
  ,, John Richards
  ,, William Richards
  ,, Morgan Rees
  ,, William Miles
  ,, Lewis Thomas
G. R. Morgan Esqre

For the Original motion

Mr D. W. James
  ,, Benjamin Martin
  ,, Henry Kirkhouse
  ,, Lewis Lewis
  ,, John Smith
  ,, George Martin
  ,, Richard Williams
  ,, Morgan Morgan
William Thomas Esqre
H. A. Bruce Esqre
C. S. Hutchins Esqre
Mr William Howell

being 11 for the ammendment and 12 for the original motion which was declared duly carried. And the Clerk was directed to forward a copy of the foregoing resolution to the Poor Law Commissioners with a request that the majority be ——— permitted to carry out the same

Resolution approving the building of a workhouse, 1848.
Minutes of the Board of Guardians.

Poor Relief
in
Merthyr Tydfil Union
in
Victorian Times

based on a study of original documents

by
TYDFIL THOMAS, O.B.E., J.P., M.A.

1992
A Glamorgan Archive Service Publication

© The Glamorgan Archive Service and the Author, 1992

ISBN 0 905243 26 9

Set in 11 on 12pt Bembo

Printed in Wales by
D. Brown and Sons Ltd., Bridgend, Mid Glamorgan

Contents

List of

Illustrations and Maps

Abbreviations

AAM	Amalgamated Association of Miners
DWB	*A Dictionary of Welsh Biography*
CMG	*Cardiff and Merthyr Guardian* newspaper
GRO	Glamorgan Record Office, Cardiff
LGB	Local Government Board
ME	*Merthyr Express* newspaper
MH	Ministry of Health records
MTBG	Merthyr Tydfil Board of Guardians
PLB	Poor Law Board
PLC	Poor Law Commission
PRO	Public Record Office, London
WHR	*The Welsh History Review*
p.a.	*per annum*, yearly

Foreword

This book examines the human suffering which lay behind the industrialisation of South Wales. Many histories emphasise the great technical advances which made possible the large-scale production of iron and steel and the development of Merthyr Tydfil as the key location of this industry in Glamorgan. Some describe the skills and tribulations of the workers, others the enterprise and ruthlessness of the masters of industry. This book, in treating of the New Poor Law, deals with the people, jobless workmen, widows, children, the aged and the sick, who, for no fault of their own, found themselves destitute, and dependent on poor relief for their very existence, and classified by the legal term of 'pauper'.

How the number of paupers increased in the second half of the nineteenth century, and how both central and local government attempted to deal with the problem, is shown by Tydfil Thomas from the vivid evidence of contemporary documents and records.

The general theme has been treated many times by historians, but here we have a specific study relating to the area covered by the Merthyr Tydfil Union. The subject has been of special interest to educationalists in the presentation of social history, and it is significant that the inspiration for the present study was generated in lectures given by Mrs. Thomas to courses of sixth-formers and teachers, held at Dyffryn House Residential Centre, St. Nicholas, by the Glamorgan County Council Education Department, many years ago. In this connection it is pertinent to recall the support and encouragement given to those ventures by Mr. A. H. Williams, H.M.I.

The present work forms a sequel to an earlier volume published by the Glamorgan Record office, *On the Parish*, written by Dr. R. K. J. Grant. In that book, the implementation of the Old Poor Law before 1834 was traced through records surviving from Glamorgan parishes and from the Court of Quarter Sessions. That volume too grew out of the Dyffryn House Local History courses which Dr. Grant organised for the County Council, and in which he also delivered lectures. The two books now complement each other.

This Foreword provides an opportunity to thank various individuals, not least the author herself, whose command of, and commitment to her subject, comes out strongly in her writing. I would wish to thank members of the Glamorgan Record Office staff for their practical assistance, notably Michael Wilcox, Ann Sefton and Colleen Abson. Lastly, I am grateful to my husband for his assistance in proof-reading, and for help in many ways while preparing these pages for the printer.

Patricia Moore
Glamorgan Archivist

Glossary

Able-bodied — Men and women who were capable of earning a living but were destitute because they could not obtain work.

Andover Scandal — The workhouse at Andover, Hampshire, was so harsh in its treatment of paupers that in 1845 the inmates, desperate for food, fought each other for the rotting bones they had to crush for fertiliser, as task work. This incident gave rise to an enquiry which revealed the truth of the allegations of harshness, cruelty and corruption.

Boarding-out — Maintaining some classes of paupers outside the workhouse.

Central Authority — The Poor Law Commissioners 1834-1847, the Poor Law Board 1847-1871, the Local Government Board 1871-1919.

Court of Requests — A court in Merthyr Tydfil created in 1809 for the recovery of small debts, technically those of less than £5. It could order the seizure of goods belonging to debtors who could not pay. It was used mainly by shop-keepers who were owed money.

Dispensaries — Places where medicines could be provided for sick paupers in times of epidemics.

Foul Wards — Hospital wards in the workhouse where paupers suffering from venereal diseases were treated.

Gruel — A mixture of oatmeal and water without the addition of sugar or milk.

House of Refuge — A place to which families of sick paupers could be sent during epidemics in order to prevent the spread of infection.

Imbeciles, idiots — People who had been born mentally ill or defective, or had become so.

Indoor relief — Poor relief given to paupers inside the workhouse.

Outdoor relief — Poor relief given either in money or in kind (mainly food), to paupers outside the workhouse.

Labour Test — Work of a hard or unpleasant nature such as stone-breaking or oakum-picking, given to able-bodied paupers as a means of testing the actual destitution of the applicant. It was also called task work.

Lock-out — The exclusion of workmen by employers from their works as a means of coercion during strikes.

Nuisances — Filth and offensive material injurious to public health.

Oakum-picking — Teasing out the coarse fibres of flax or hemp or obtaining them by the unravelling of old rope. An unpleasant task which chafed the skin and left the hands and fingers raw and bleeding.

Sale coal, sea coal — The coal mined for sale or for export.

Steam coal	Coal mined in South Wales which was in demand for its smokeless quality and steam-raising powers.
Surgeon	In the context of the Union, the name applied to doctors who carried out medical duties such as attending sick paupers.
Task work	See Labour Test.
Union	The grouping of parishes as a Union for the administration of poor relief after the introduction of the Poor Law Amendment Act of 1834.
Unitarians	Members of a nonconformist religious group holding radical views in religion and politics.
Utilitarianism	The theory that an action is right if it achieves the greatest good for the greatest number of people. The philosophers Jeremy Bentham and John Stuart Mill gave a full defence of this theory.
Vagrants	Tramps and their followers who wandered about the country begging, with no serious intention of finding work.
Vestry	A meeting of rate-payers of a parish for the purpose of transacting parish business such as the setting of the poor rate for the relief of the poor.
Workhouse	The institution which provided accommodation, food and care for paupers in return for the (unpaid) work of which they were capable.

Notes on Money

Sums of money were expressed in the documents in currency of the period, based on pounds, shillings and pence. The following table enumerates the old denominations:

2 farthings	= 1 halfpenny ($\frac{1}{2}$d.)		20 shillings	= 1 pound (£1)
4 farthings	= 1 penny (1d.)		21 shillings	= 1 guinea (1gn.)
12 pennies	= 1 shilling (1s. or 1/-)		10 shillings & 6 pence	
2 shillings	= 1 florin (2s. 0d. or 2/-)			= half a guinea
2 shillings & 6 pence				
	= 1 half-crown (2s. 6d. or 2/6)			

The purchasing power of all denominations has declined through the years, and is therefore much less today than it was in the last century. Comparisons with current values are inevitably misleading owing to changing standards of living, and even if modern equivalents were estimated in the text, they would quickly become out-of-date. Consequently, the old denominations have been quoted without any attempt to suggest a modern equivalent.

Decimal currency was introduced in 1971. The £1 denomination was retained (the florin and half-crown were abolished), and the pound divided into 100 pennies (instead of the previous 240); thus the old 6d. equals 2$\frac{1}{2}$ decimal pence, and so on.

Acknowledgements

I wish to acknowledge my indebtedness to Mrs. Patricia Moore, the Glamorgan Archivist, for her help and encouragement in preparing this work. It is one of a series of publications under her editorship, brought out by the Glamorgan Archives Joint Committee, which has borne the main cost. A grant by the Welsh Office and assistance from Mid Glamorgan County Council have also been received, and this generous support is warmly acknowledged.

It has been a pleasure to work at the Glamorgan Record Office in Cardiff, at the Welsh Industrial and Maritime Museum, the Central Library, Cardiff, Merthyr Tydfil Public Library, Aberdare Public Library and at Cyfarthfa Castle Museum, where members of staff in every case have been extremely helpful. For her patience and forbearance, my gratitude goes to Ms. P. Rowburrey who typed the manuscript, and to Mr. Meirion Davies who prepared the index.

My thanks are also due to Mr. Alun Baldwin who took the modern photographs of St. Tydfil's Hospital, so as to record surviving evidence of the building which once had been the workhouse.

I have to thank Dr. Dorothy Marshall, my original mentor and inspiration in the subject of poor law. I also wish to thank Emeritus Professor Ieuan Gwynedd Jones who offered invaluable advice in the early stages of the preparation of this book. I have to acknowledge my deep gratitude to Mr. David Maddox, General Adviser in History for Mid Glamorgan, for his interest and practical support. I would also like to thank the firm of D. Brown and Sons of Cowbridge and Bridgend, for their excellent work in the printing of this book.

Any defects or shortcomings are entirely my own responsibility, but I hope the spirit of the subject has been captured, because it is something very dear to my heart.

Tydfil Thomas

Preface

This publication shows how poor relief was administered in the Merthyr Tydfil Poor Law Union between 1834 and 1894, under the terms of the Poor Law Amendment Act of 1834. The subject draws on a rich arrary of source material, both primary and secondary. The minute books of the Board of Guardians provide the major source of evidence for an examination of how this form of poor relief operated, and they also illustrate the forces at work behind it. It has been necessary to draw upon wider resources and on the records of central government to give the subject fuller treatment. Quotations from these primary sources have been included in the text so as to show the nature of the documentary material. To assist the researcher, document references have been included in the text.

This examination, as well as shedding light on how the system of poor relief operated locally, also reflects the national influences at work. In Merthyr Tydfil Union the forces of rapid industrialisation and enormous social change underlie the theme of poor relief, giving it dramatic impact. Not only have the practicalities of dealing with poor relief to be considered, but also the underlying influence of ironmasters, coal-owners, and property-owners, all of whom, as rate-payers, were conditioned by the political, economic and social philosophy of the time.

The politics of poverty is a subtle theme. Gwyn A. Williams has shown how radicalism and Unitarianism became powerful influences in Merthyr Tydfil; Ieuan Gwynedd Jones has carried the exploration further forward into the politics of the area in the 1860s.

This publication gives specific evidence of the ways in which the poor were relieved in an area which, for a brief period, enjoyed the status of the iron metropolis of the world. The work should encourage students and general readers to explore for themselves the records of the Merthyr Tydfil Union, and of other Unions, held in County Record Offices.

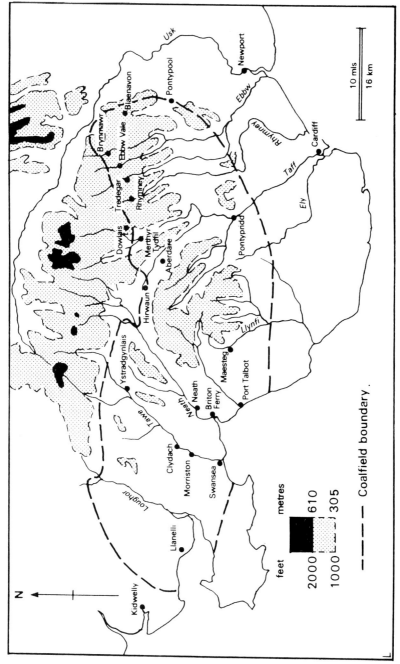

A map of the industrial areas of South Wales in the early nineteenth century. Published in *People, Protest and Politics* by David Egan.

CHAPTER 1

The Klondike of Wales

An examination of poor relief in north-east Glamorgan in the area of Merthyr
Tydfil Poor Law Union between 1834 and 1894 reveals in a most dramatic way
the powerful economic, social and political changes which took place in this
area in the nineteenth century. By 1831, with a population of 22,083, Merthyr
Tydfil was the largest town in Wales and by the mid 1840s was fast becoming
the iron metropolis of the world. Further rapid increases in the population
continued until 1851, after which the rate of growth slowed down.

Its neighbour, the parish of Aberdare, in 1831, had a population of only 3,961
but then experienced a tremendous surge of growth from 1831 to 1861, the
population doubling every ten years, the greatest expansion taking place in the
decade 1851-1861 when it increased by 18,000 (see Appendix 1). Both these
towns were founded on iron, and both developed the sale coal trade (coal for
general sale) as the iron industry declined. The high wages that could be earned
in these industries were the major attraction to immigrants who came initially
from Glamorgan, Breconshire and counties further west. A post-war
depression in agriculture compelled them to go in search of work after 1815,
and the constant demand for labour in Merthyr and Aberdare valleys lured
people in that direction. For the same reasons, from the 1840s, there was a
steady movement of Irish immigrants and of people from rural counties across
the Bristol Channel.

IRON

Since the middle of the eighteenth century, English industrialists such as
Anthony Bacon had looked towards South Wales for the production of iron,
which was essential for Britain in time of war. South Wales had much to offer:
plentiful supplies of iron ore, cheap fuel (first wood and then coal), limestone
for smelting and abundant supplies of water. The most important centre was
Merthyr Tydfil where, in 1759, the Dowlais Iron Company was founded. This
was followed by the development of the Plymouth Works, the Cyfarthfa
Works and the Penydarren Works. Owing to the absence of industrial capital in
Wales, the ironworks were developed by capitalists from England who
established great industrial dynasties: the Crawshays at Cyfarthfa and Hirwaun,
the Guests at Dowlais, the Hills at Plymouth, the Homfrays at Penydarren and
the Fothergills at Abernant, Aberdare. For a brief period, first the Cyfarthfa
Works and then the Dowlais Works were the largest in the world. Great

William Crawshay II.
(The Cyfarthfa Ironworks and Cyfarthfa Castle are shown in the background.)

expansion occurred in the Welsh iron industry during the Napoleonic Wars, and, for 50 years after, it remained the dominant element in the economy of South Wales.

The development of railways after the effective adoption of steam locomotion in 1825 led to an enormous demand for iron rails. Those for the Stockton-Darlington Railway were made at the Dowlais Works, while the rails for the Liverpool to Manchester Railway were manufactured at Penydarren. The railway boom of the 1830s and 1840s was fully exploited by both the Dowlais and Cyfarthfa Works which were at their peak. Lady Charlotte Guest mentioned in her diary in 1844 that the Dowlais Iron Company made a contract to supply 50,000 tons of rails to Russia, this order being the largest of its kind ever to be arranged. In November 1845, she calculated that the output from the Dowlais Works was 1,100 tons of rails and 130 tons of bars per week, which was a greater quantity than any other works could produce (Bessborough, 1952, p. 171).

Dowlais Works provided rails for the Baltimore and Susquehanna Railway, the Berlin and Leipzig Railway, the St Petersburg-Pauloffsky Railway and the New Orleans and Nashville Railway. Rails for the East India Company were supplied by both the Dowlais and Cyfarthfa Iron Works (Hayman, 1989, p. 12). At home, in the face of fierce competition, these two companies

2

captured orders for the supply of rails. The Midland, York and North Midland, Preston and Wyre, and Eastern Counties Railways were supplied by the Cyfarthfa Works, while those of the Great Western, South Eastern, the Dover and Eastern Counties Railways were supplied by the Dowlais Works.

COAL

The prosperity of the iron industry was dependent upon an abundant supply of cheap coal with the result that the ironmasters opened new levels and pits. The mining of coal for sale also became important, though initially it was not in the hands of the ironmasters but of small local developers. In 1824, Robert Thomas opened a level at Waun Wyllt near Merthyr Tydfil and developed the famous 'Four-Feet Seam' from which he supplied coal to householders at Merthyr and

Merthyr Tydfil in the 1840s.

Cardiff (Morris & Williams, 1958, p. 19). He, together with George Insole, gained entry into the London market where there was a great demand for Welsh steam coal. On the death of Robert Thomas, his widow, Lucy, and her son continued this trade at Abercanaid, gaining her the title of 'The Mother of the Welsh Steam Coal Trade'. Until 1840, her coal was the only steam coal shipped from Cardiff, the other major shipments being the house coal produced by Walter Coffin at Dinas in the Rhondda Valley and by Thomas Powell at Gelligaer.

In the 1840s, the opening of collieries in the Aberdare Valley led to a major expansion in the steam coal trade. In 1837, the Waynes with others opened a pit at Cwmbach, Aberdare, where they struck the Four-Feet Seam, which enabled them to provide steam coal for export. Thomas Powell sank five pits during the 1840s, including two at Duffryn, thereby later originating the name Powell Duffryn. David Williams of Ynyscynon, David Davis of Blaengwawr, John Nixon of Werfa and Crawshay Bailey of Aberaman were all involved in the sale of coal trade, and, most of the coal exported from Cardiff at this time came from the Aberdare and Merthyr Valleys.

An ironworks by night. Watercolour by Thomas Hornor of 1819.

TRANSPORT

The development of means of communication was crucial to the iron and coal industries if wider markets for their products were to be reached. The initiative was first taken by Anthony Bacon of the Cyfarthfa Ironworks in 1767 when a road was constructed along the Taff Valley and later improved by the Turnpike Trust. Iron was brought down to the coast in wagons drawn by horses, each wagon carrying two tons, but this was a slow and expensive procedure so the search for improved transport continued. Again, the owners of the Cyfarthfa Ironworks took the lead. Merthyr ironmasters raised the capital to build a canal down to Cardiff and applied to Parliament for an enabling Act. Richard Crawshay provided the largest share of the capital. By 1794, the canal was completed, the head being extended to the Cyfarthfa Works, to the obvious advantage of Crawshay. The 25 miles covered by this canal involved a fall of 543 feet between Merthyr and Cardiff, and required 51 locks. Along the canal went an endless procession of barges, each carrying 24 tons of iron and each pulled by a horse and controlled by a man and a boy. To meet the need of the Aberdare ironworks, a branch canal along the Cynon Valley was constructed in 1811 joining the Glamorganshire Canal at Abercynon.

Despite the financial success of this venture, there were many difficulties associated with it. The proprietors of the Dowlais, Penydarren and Plymouth Works therefore decided to build a tramroad from Penydarren to Abercynon in 1802, on which horse-drawn trams were used, each tram containing 10 tons of iron. It was on this famous tramroad that Richard Trevithick ran his high pressure steam engine in 1804 from the Penydarren Works down to Abercynon, but this epoch-making run was an isolated event and the Taff Vale Railway from Merthyr Tydfil to Cardiff was not built until 1841.

The Glamorganshire Canal was already becoming obsolete when the railway age arrived. Josiah John Guest took the lead by inviting the engineer Isambard Kingdom Brunel, to make a survey in 1834 for a railway from Merthyr Tydfil to Cardiff, and a company was formed to build the Taff Vale Railway. Though the Canal Company strongly resisted an Act of Parliament authorising the railway, and received compensation for loss of trade, the railway was built. It was completed by 1841 and an extension along the Cynon Valley to Aberdare was added in 1846. Thus the stage was set for the exploitation of steam coal measures in these valleys, and, after 1865, in the Rhondda Valleys, so that by the end of the century Cardiff became the steam-coal metropolis of the world.

ECONOMIC, SOCIAL AND POLITICAL CONSEQUENCES

Among the inevitable consequences of industrial expansion in the early stages of capitalist growth were the periodic fluctuations in trade and industry known as the 'trade cycle'. The slump which occurred in 1848 was particularly bad, the gloom being intensified by revolution abroad and discontent at home. In the iron and coal industries, the rise and fall in prosperity was reflected in wages, since the market price of iron and coal was the indicator which determined wages. Reductions in pay were not accepted without opposition by the workers, who found that their employers were reluctant and unwilling to recognise trade unions. Professor Ieuan Gwynedd Jones has pointed out the powerful, all-consuming nature of the ironmasters' oligarchy in Merthyr Tydfil and has contrasted their entrenched power with the weakness and disorientation of immigrants within these industrial empires. (Jones, 1987, pp. 350-353). In earlier industrial disputes, workmen tried to organise unions, but strong trade unionism was slow to develop. There was a display of militancy by the Aberdare colliers in 1850 and 1857, and also the formation of the Glamorgan Union of Colliers, but not until the 1870s was there a real show of strength. The formation of the Amalgamated Association of Miners, the Trade Union Acts of 1871 and 1875 and three major strikes between 1871 and 1875, were necessary before effective trade unionism could emerge.

The period prior to the introduction of the New Poor Law was one of great political and economic unrest. The Reform Bill agitation coincided with an economic slump and produced a dramatic crisis. In Merthyr Tydfil, unemployment, falling wages, a bankrupt Vestry, and a savage Court of

Henry Richard.

Requests (see glossary), built up such tension at this time of reform, that it only needed the inflammatory oratory of the great meeting held in early June 1831 on the Waun above Dowlais to cause the crowds to erupt into violence. The Court of Requests was a tangible target which the rioters could attack: its premises were sacked, its records destroyed and the goods which had been confiscated from poor people for small debts were restored to their original owners. The unforgettable experience of the riots, and the tragic aftermath of the trials in the Glamorgan Assizes, became a legend in people's minds. Professor Gwyn A. Williams has summed up their importance: '*They* [the riots] *were one of those surface cataclysms which signify a profound shift in depths . . . For the working class movement in South Wales, this was the point of emergence*'. (Glanmor Williams, 1966, p. 25. See also Gwyn A. Williams, 1978).

A mass meeting of the locked-out at Mountain Hare, Merthyr Tydfil. Drawn for *The Illustrated London News*, 1875.

The Reform Act of 1832 gave Wales five additional parliamentary seats, one of which was the parliamentary borough of Merthyr Tydfil covering Aberdare, Merthyr Tydfil and Vaynor with Cefn Coed-y-Cymmer. Only men over the age of 21 holding property rated at £10 yearly and above, exercised the vote. In an area with over 40,000 inhabitants most of whom occupied rented accommodation, only about 520 men, mainly industrialists, traders and shopkeepers, qualified for a vote. The power of the ironmasters remained supreme and it is, therefore, not surprising that the first Member for the parliamentary borough should have been Josiah John Guest.

In the same way, ironmasters and middle-class voters exercised powerful control over the Board of Guardians when they were elected in 1836. Professor

Ieuan Gwynedd Jones has pointed out that voting was distributed according to a strict system of classification by wealth, which was true also for Public Health matters after 1848. Furthermore, the property qualification for Guardians was high (£500 in real property or a private income of at least £15 a year). He states, '*This is why the Boards so elected were representative mainly of middle-class property owners rather than the £8 ratepayers and were consequently easily dominated and controlled by the industrial or monied interests*' (Jones, 1987, p.347). This remained so until local government reforms at the end of the century.

By 1867, in the constituency of Merthyr Tydfil, only one man in 57 had the vote and, in the coalfields, where population was most densely concentrated, the workers were excluded from political power. The militants in the working class turned to Chartism as a means of redress and reform, and one of the arch enemies of the Chartists was the New Poor Law with its 'Bastilles', as the workhouses were called. In face of Chartist militancy and the fear of wholesale insurrection, it is understandable that penny-pinching Guardians should have deliberately delayed the provision of a workhouse and should have fallen back on the easier solution of perpetuating outdoor relief for as long as possible.

Politically, the turning-point came in 1868 when, as a result of the Reform Act of 1867, the electorate in Merthyr Tydfil parliamentary borough leapt from 1,387 to 14,577 and gained an additional member of parliament. The Act extended the right to vote, with certain qualifications, to male householders. H. A. Bruce, who had succeeded Guest, lost his seat, and at the top of the poll was Henry Richard, a man with no industrial or commercial connections, but who was a Welshman, a Liberal and a nonconformist, known as 'the Apostle of Peace'. He even outran Richard Fothergill, a Liberal industrialist, who was the other elected member. Nonconformist radicalism was now a political force to be reckoned with, but it took the Ballot Act of 1872 and another Reform Act in 1884 before Britain could claim to be a democracy.

CHAPTER 2

The New Poor Law
and its background

The economic and social changes brought about by the Industrial Revolution produced acute problems, of which poverty and lack of public health provision were among the most serious. The Reformed Parliament of 1832 directed its immediate attention to reforming the Poor Law.

THE OLD POOR LAW

The 'Old Poor Law' was based on the famous Poor Law of 1601 which had been enacted to meet a different set of social conditions. It had placed the responsibility of looking after the poor on each ecclesiastical parish and this duty was discharged by the parishioners who met as a parish Vestry. The Vestry determined the poor rate which was usually fixed quarterly, with all ratepayers paying so much in the pound according to the value of their property. This continued for more than 200 years, the parish being responsible not only for looking after the poor, but also for the roads and the maintenance of the church. By the early years of the nineteenth century, the greatest ratepayers in the parishes of Aberdare and Merthyr Tydfil were the owners of the ironworks and coalmines. They dominated these Vestries and no decisions of any real importance were taken unless they or their agents were present.

Crucial to the working of the Old Poor Law were the overseers of the poor, who, with the churchwardens, saw to the collection of the poor rate and its disbursement. Chosen from farmers and men of good standing in the parish, the overseers held office for a year and were unpaid. Their account books were examined by the parish Vestry or its agents (Grant, 1988, pp. 37-42). Most payments to paupers were in money or in kind, but parish poorhouses or workhouses could be provided. The former were meant to protect the impotent (helpless) poor and the latter were intended as a deterrent to the work-shy, able-bodied poor; both types of institution varied greatly according to time and place.

The administration of poor relief under the Old Poor Law was further complicated by the Law of Settlement of 1662. According to this law, any person coming into a parish where he or she had no legal 'settlement' could be arrested and taken before a Justice of the Peace for examination. A settlement could be gained by being born in a parish, by serving an apprenticeship there, by being hired as a servant for a year, by paying local rates or by serving as one of the parish officers. Wives gained settlement by marriage. This system was modified in 1794 so that people could not be examined unless they applied for poor relief or were caught begging. An Order of Removal could be issued by a Justice of the Peace after a pauper had been examined on oath, so that he or she could be sent back to the parish which was legally responsible for maintenance. Irish paupers were removed under the Vagrancy Acts since there was no such place as a legal settlement in Irish Law (Grant, 1988, p. 53). The outcome of this Act was a great deal of hardship for paupers and also much litigation over matters of settlement.

The greatest problem facing parish Vestries was that of the able-bodied poor who were willing to work but had very low wages. The Berkshire magistrates had in 1795 worked out a scale of relief to supplement wages according to the price of corn and the size of the family. This system was not applied in Wales in such a precise form, but income subsidies were certainly paid in Aberdare parish (Davies, 1977, p. 293). The Overseers treated each application individually but had regard to the size of the family and the cost of food. Because of the industrial expansion in this area in the 1820s, there was less need for poor relief for the able-bodied than in agricultural areas. Some historians now believe that the Old Poor Law worked well, despite its amateur administration, unsatisfactory method of finance and alleged abuses. It is argued that the demoralising effects of wage subsidies were less harmful than ratepayers or commissioners asserted (Davies, 1977, discusses this approach).

Yet by the 1830s, the progressive increase of pauperism nationally, and the vast human problems created by rapid industrialisation, placed excessive burdens on parish Vestries which were never intended to deal with poverty on such a scale or of such complexity as that which resulted from trade recessions. This is well illustrated by the emergency that overtook Merthyr Tydfil Vestry in 1830 when it became completely insolvent (Grant, 1988, p. 62. See also Gwyn A. Williams, 1978, p. 60).

THE ROYAL COMMISSION ON THE POOR LAWS, 1832

The problem of the able-bodied poor reached such proportions nationally as to create panic. Even before the passing of the Reform Act of 1832, a Royal Commission on the Poor Laws had been appointed. One of the Assistant Commissioners was Edwin Chadwick, an ardent Benthamite and influential Poor Law and Public Health reformer who played a major part in the preparation of the Poor Law Report of 1834. This Report exposed the weaknesses and inefficiency of the existing system and recommended that there should be a new rigour in the administration of poor relief. Whatever criticism may be levelled against it, the Report was essentially the product of the social attitudes of its time, and the two principles it recommended were in accordance with prevailing beliefs: 'the workhouse test' and 'less eligibility' were to be the basis of the New Poor Law.

By 'the workhouse test', all outdoor relief to the able-bodied and their families was to be abolished. No able-bodied man should obtain relief unless he and his family entered the workhouse. This appeared in the first recommendation of the Report: '*That except as to Medical Attendance, and subject to the exception respecting apprenticeship hereinafter stated, all relief whatever to able-bodied persons, or to their families, otherwise than in well-regulated workhouses (i.e. places where they may be set to work according to the spirit and intention of the 43rd of Elizabeth) shall be declared unlawful, and shall cease, in manner and at periods hereafter specified*' (*Report of the Royal Commission for inquiring into the Administration and Practical Operation of the Poor Laws*, 1834, XXVII, p. 146).

Edwin Chadwick (1800–1890).
Drawn for *The Illustrated London News*, 1848.

According to the principle of 'less eligibility', the assistance provided for the person in need had to be such as to cause his condition to be less desirable or satisfactory than the condition of the lowest paid labourer not in receipt of poor relief. Thus paupers receiving poor relief inside workhouses would receive the kind of treatment which made their condition infinitely less preferable than that of the lowest paid workers outside. This did not mean that the food and material conditions of paupers in the workhouse would reach the lowest possible point of existence, but it did mean that the discipline of the workhouse would make it an intolerable place to indolent and disorderly people. The emphasis on monotonous routine, irksome tasks and strong discipline were the hallmarks of the workhouse system. Inmates were segregated according to age and sex, and workhouses were made 'as prison-like as possible' in order to inspire fear and dread. This caused them to become places of 'unresolvable tension', as it was difficult to see how they could deter the able-bodied poor while, at the same time, provide a refuge for the sick, aged and helpless poor. (See Crowther, 1983, pp. 40-42).

'Less eligibility' had not been laid down as a recommendation but occurred as an assertion in an argument in the Report, yet this was the principle that was to dominate the administration of poor relief for the next 75 years. The

St. Tydfil's Hospital, formerly the Union workhouse, photographed in 1992.

workhouse was to be the mechanism through which the doctrine of 'less eligibility' should be carried out, and with the defects of mixed workhouses in mind, the Commissioners advised segregation in separate workhouses, according to age and sex. '*We recommend that the Central Board be empowered to cause any number of parishes which they think convenient to be incorporated for the purpose of workhouse management, and to assign to those workhouses separate classes of poor, though composed of the poor of distinct parishes, each distinct parish paying to the support of the permanent workhouse establishment*' (Report, 1834, XXVII, p. 176).

Commenting on these two principles, Professor S. E. Finer has pointed out that 'less eligibility' proved to be a political economist's abstraction. It was a vague principle, admitting infinite degrees of administrative discretion. 'The workhouse test' could only be carried out at enormous expense, and once this was proved, Boards of Guardians were reluctant to adopt it. Finer summed up the position by stating that '*The two supposedly self-acting principles turned out to be very hit-or-miss affairs*' (Finer, 1952, p. 86).

But more important than these statements of abstract principles were the administrative changes recommended by the Commissioners. '*We recommend, therefore, the appointment of a Central Board to control the administration of the Poor Laws, with such Assistant Commissioners as may be found requisite; and that the Commissioners be empowered and directed to frame and enforce regulations for the government of workhouses, and as to the nature and amount of relief to be given, and the labour to be exacted in them, and that such regulations shall as far as may be practicable, be uniform throughout the country*' (Report, 1834, XXVII, p. 167). This recommendation has been described as embodying the most revolutionary principle of the Poor Law Report. At last there was to be national uniformity in the treatment of each class of paupers under the supervision of a central authority. After more than two hundred years of extreme localism, national supervision and larger administrative units were to be introduced which meant a revolution in Poor Law administration. The parish with its potential for corruption and inefficiency was to be replaced by a unified system under central control. Professor Finer summed up these proposals: '*They have proved the source of nearly all the important developments in English local government viz, central supervision, central inspection, central audit, a professional government service controlled by local elective bodies and the adjustment of areas to administrative exigencies*' (Finer, 1952, p. 88).

With all its shortcomings, the Poor Law Report of 1834 can be regarded as one of the classic documents of western social history and one which reflected contemporary social philosophy. To Malthus and his followers, to the Benthamites and the supporters of Adam Smith, poverty was a condition which should be relieved publicly only as a last resort. The burden of destitution should be placed firmly on the shoulders of the individual, who through some moral fault, was responsible for his condition. '*Laissez-faire*' was the doctrine of this age of middle-class supremacy which believed that the State should interfere as little as possible with private interests. Poor relief was regarded as a drain on the pockets of the rich through the rates, and was believed to be a threat to the State because it bred potential revolutionaries.

Reflecting these views, the members of the Commission made no attempt to enquire into the causes of poverty, but simply concentrated their attention on the system of granting relief. For this fundamental reason, their diagnosis of the problem of poverty was flawed, and the remedies they proposed were inadequate.

THE POOR LAW AMENDMENT ACT, 1834

The Report was introduced into Parliament on 13 April, 1834, and a Bill embodying its proposals was introduced on 17 April; it was passed on 13 August and was given the Royal Assent on 14 August 1834. Entitled '*An Act for the Amendment and better Administration of the Laws relating to the Poor of England and Wales*', it adopted the spirit and principles of the Report without clearly defining them. Its main feature was the administrative machinery that it created. It provided for the appointment of three Poor Law Commissioners to form a Central Advisory Board. They were to choose a paid Secretary and Assistant Secretary, and were empowered to appoint nine Assistant Commissioners. From this Central Poor Law Department were issued orders and regulations to guide the local Poor Law officers. Locally, the orders of the Commissioners were to be carried out by Boards of Guardians elected by the ratepayers of parishes grouped together into Unions for the purpose. The Guardians appointed officers to serve them, subject to the approval of the Commissioners.

The Poor Law Commission was not given representation in Parliament and, therefore, knew no direct control and had no direct protection. This was a victory for the followers of Jeremy Bentham, the political philosopher, whose ideas for the reform of law, political institutions and morals had a major influence in shaping the New Poor Law, the Public Health movement and other public institutions. Benthamism, especially its ethical teaching, is sometimes synonymous with Utilitarianism, and the New Poor Law was Utilitarian both in its conception and its execution. A group of three Commissioners was considered more efficient and more flexible than a department controlled by Parliament. The Poor Law Commission was to influence the Unions by presenting them with information and persuading them to act upon it, rather than by exercising arbitary power. Time proved that in the absence of coercive powers, the central authority could make the Guardians initiate nothing. As the Royal Commission of 1904 pointed out in relation to the central authority, its powers of prohibition were great, but those of initiation were small.

The Poor Law Commission, with Chadwick as Secretary, was in being from 1834 to 1847, by which time it had become fatally weakened, especially after the Andover Scandal (see glossary). It was replaced by the Poor Law Board which consisted of five members of the Privy Council including a President and his Parliamentary Secretary, both of whom were Members of Parliament. The Poor Law Board did not show the zeal of the Commissioners and allowed its leadership to flag. It made no attempt to bring general policy into conformity

Jeremy Bentham (1748-1832).
Bentham's clothed skeleton, prepared in accordance with his instructions, and given a wax head,
is displayed at University College, London.

with the Poor Law Report of 1834, mainly because of the difficulty that had been experienced in operating its principles up to 1847. It replaced the title of Assistant Commissioner with that of Poor Law Inspector, and provision was made for the appointment of two Inspectors for Poor Law schools.

In 1871, the Poor Law Board was merged into the Local Government Board which also took over the growing Public Health service. The Local Government Board consisted of a President, Parliamentary Secretary and three permanent secretaries. Established on a more permanent basis, it showed increasing confidence in the way in which it dealt with Boards of Guardians. Between 1871 and 1885 there was a constant effort on the part of a somewhat doctrinaire inspectorate to enforce *the principles of 1834*. The outstanding feature of the policy of the Local Government Board during these years was the attempt to reduce outdoor relief. This policy was implemented by Boards of Guardians who were representative of propertied interests which were anxious to keep down poor rates regardless of personal suffering. Their conscious concern was with the moral character of the destitute which they saw threatened by the grant of poor relief. While outdoor relief could not be abolished, the number of people cared for by the Boards of Guardians fell by the end of the 1870s. Though the right to poor relief existed, people got along without it for as long as they possibly could.

A view of Dowlais works. Watercolour by Childs, 1840s.

CHAPTER 3

The application of the New Poor Law in Merthyr Tydfil Union

In accordance with the terms of the Act the Poor Law Commissioners began by dividing England and Wales into nine areas, for each of which they appointed an Assistant Commissioner, whose duties were to group parishes into Unions and arrange the election of Boards of Guardians. George Clive was the Assistant Commissioner in charge of Monmouth, Carmarthen, Glamorgan and part of Gloucester. In his report for 1836, he stated that he had formed seven Unions in his district but none of them had yet come into operation. Referring to reaction to the new Act, he believed that the general opinion in Monmouthshire, Glamorgan and parts of Gloucestershire, was that no advantage could be gained from its introduction. This opinion was based mainly on the absence of able-bodied pauperism in the area, which he attributed to the immense demand for labour and the high wages paid in industrial areas. However, he considered the parochial system was as inefficient in his district as elsewhere mainly because of its inherent weaknesses (*The Second Report of the Poor Law Commissioners*, 1836, p. 394).

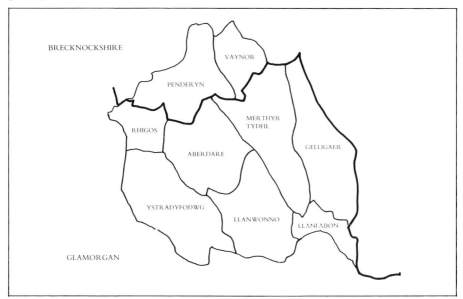

Diagram map of the parishes within the Merthyr Tydfil Union.

Assistant Commissioner Clive visited Merthyr Tydfil early in May 1836, to make preliminary enquiries about forming a Union (*Cardiff and Merthyr Guardian*, 7 May 1836). He considered including the parishes of Merthyr Tydfil, Aberdare, Gelligaer, Eglwysilan, Llanfabon, Llanwonno and Ystradyfodwg (in the old county of Glamorgan) as well as Penderyn and Vaynor (in the old county of Breconshire). By September 1836, he had decided that there should be twenty Guardians for Merthyr Tydfil Union which would cover a population of about 50,000. The nine parishes making up the Union and the rate at which they were assessed were made known in October.

TABLE 1

PARISH	NUMBER OF GUARDIANS	PROPORTION
Merthyr Tydfil... ...	8	£4,019
Aberdare..	3	£948
Gelligaer..	2	£615
Llanwonno	1	£376
Llanfabon	1	£325
Ystradyfodwg	2	£302 £446
Rhigos		£144
Penderyn	2	£439
Vaynor	2	£378

(*CMG* 29 Oct. 1836).

The first meeting of the Board of Guardians for Merthyr Tydfil Union was held at The Castle Inn, Merthyr Tydfil, on 3 November 1836, when the result of the election was announced.

As has already been pointed out, the property qualification for the voting system under the New Poor Law ensured that the Board of Guardians was representative of the propertied middle class; it was consequently dominated by industrial and monied interests. At their first meeting on 3 November 1836, Josiah John Guest took the chair initially until J. B. Bruce, a landowner, stipendiary magistrate and well-known opponent of the Poor Law Amendment Act, was elected chairman through the influence of Thompson, an ironmaster and Meyrick a lawyer. D. W. James, a radical reformer and member of the influential James dynasty, was elected as vice-chairman with the backing of Guest and the radicals. The James family originated with Christopher James who came from Whitchurch, near Cardiff, and was the spokesman of the carriers on the Glamorganshire Canal. His eldest son, D. W. James, was 'the grey eminence' of local politics, and his brother Job James (a former surgeon and later a bookseller), was a follower of the writer William Cobbett. Around this family grew up an influential circle connected by marriage, kinship and business. As Professor Williams points out, '*They were rational, they were calculators, and they were radicals*'. Their Unitarianism and political radicalism

Sir Josiah John Guest. Oil painting by Richard Buckner.

TABLE 2
ELECTION OF BOARD OF GUARDIANS

FOR MERTHYR TYDFIL PARISH			VOTES
Richard Jenkins, Abervan [Auctioneer].	...	...	617
Benjamin Martin, Penydarren, [Agent].	...	...	546
D. W. James [Tanner]	...	...	542
William Jones [Draper & Grocer] ...	...	...	526
Thomas Evans, Dowlais, [Agent] ...	...	...	470
Rowland Hopkins	...	...	451
William Purnell, Dowlais [?Chandler]...	...	...	371
Thomas Shepherd, Cyfarthfa, [Agent] ..	...	...	421

FOR GELLIGAER PARISH

Lewis Edwards, Bedlinog
William Evans, Llancaiach

FOR ABERDARE PARISH

Rowland Fothergill Esq., [Ironmaster]
Philip Taylor
Richard Williams, [Auctioneer]

FOR YSTRADYFODWG

William Davies

FOR RHIGOS

Morgan Philip

FOR LLANWONNO

Lewis Morgan, Esq.

FOR PENDERYN

John Thomas
William Williams, Clynperfydd

FOR VAYNOR

William Meyrick, [Solicitor]
William Williams, Penradin

FOR LLANFABON

No return

EX-OFFICIO GUARDIANS

J. B. Bruce, Esq.
J. J. Guest, Esq., M.P.
W. Thompson, Esq., M.P.
William Thomas, Esq. [of the Court estate]
Morgan Morgan, Esq.
Rev. Charles Maybery
William Morgan, Esq.

(*CMG* 5 Nov. 1836).

had a profound influence on local politics and gave them a strong foothold in the new Board of Guardians (Gwyn A. Williams, 1978, pp. 57-64).

The appointment of local officers to administer poor relief was dealt with, the office of Clerk to the Board of Guardians, a responsible position, being filled by J. W. Edwards who had previously been the Paying Officer under the pre-1834 system. For the distribution of relief, the Union was divided into three districts, each with a Relieving Officer (Minutes MTBG, 12 Nov. 1836). The first district consisted of Merthyr Tydfil and Vaynor, and was entrusted to Roger Williams at an annual salary of £100 in recognition of the greater amount of work he had to do in such a densely populated parish as Merthyr Tydfil. The second district consisted of Gelligaer, Llanfabon and Llanwonno under the control of William Jones as Relieving Officer with a salary of £70. In the third district, consisting of Ystradyfodwg (in the Rhondda valley), Rhigos, Aberdare and Penderyn, the Relieving Officer was John Williams with a salary of £70. David Evans was appointed treasurer, and three surgeons (doctors) were engaged to cover the three districts. To provide the Union with funds for the ensuing quarter, a call of £6 per cent was made, estimated to yield £7,546 (Minutes MTBG, 3 Dec. 1836). An examination of the pauper lists was carried through and completed by the Board of Guardians by 7 January 1837, and the overseers were informed that the relieving officers would supersede them on 9 January 1837. (See Appendix 2).

The Assistant Commissioner who attended the first meeting on 3 November 1836 was anxious that from the outset the Guardians should be warned of the weaknesses of the old system of poor relief and the need to reform. Aware that there was a great deal of opposition to the idea of a workhouse, he decided to expound the Poor Law Amendment Act (*CMG* 12 Nov. 1836). He stated that its objects were threefold: '*First, to compel all the able to support themselves, their children and their aged parents when work and wages were sufficient. Secondly, to teach the young, the active and the prosperous that prudence and providence are virtues well worthy of their attention, and that it is no less disgraceful to themselves than burdensome to the ratepayer to look forward to the parish purse as a pension. Thirdly, to supersede the imperfect and uncertain management of the overseers by a strong board, concentrating within itself as much intelligence and respectability as possible*'. These statements echoed the philosophy underlying the 1834 Act.

Realising that the workhouse was at the centre of the new system, he went on to expound its virtues. He emphasised that it need not be a place of torment, or a prison, and that all the poor would not be ordered into it at once, as some people believed. '*For the old, the helpless and the destitute, the workhouse would become a place of refuge and comfort; for the idle and the dissolute, it would be a punishment. The Board of Guardians would be able to consider each case individually and decide whom to order into the workhouse ... In all the unions where it was in operation (among them the neighbouring ones of Abergavenny and Monmouth), it had resulted in an immediate and considerable reduction in the rates, greater comfort for the deserving and disabled poor, and an improvement in the morals and habits of the lower classes. For these reasons, he urged the Guardians to undertake with caution and moderation, as well as with firmness and decision, their new duties under the new system*' (*CMG* 12 Nov. 1836).

Little heed was paid to this advice. Not only were the memories of the 1831 riots still fresh in the minds of those responsible for administering poor relief, but the high cost of introducing such an unpopular institution into an area where work for the able-bodied was readily available, made the Guardians very reluctant to build a workhouse. Time and events proved the Merthyr Tydfil Board to be a stubborn, intractable body which clung tenaciously to the old ways of administering poor relief, often carrying out their heavy duties in a defiant and dilatory manner. Poor Law Commissioners could cajole the Guardians about a workhouse for the next twelve years, but without success; eventually, the enormous problems caused by epidemics and heavy unemployment provided the most convincing arguments that one should be built. The Merthyr Tydfil Union showed how a system of central inspection and control might have been good in principle, but where Unions were very large, and the workload of an Assistant Commissioner was too great, centralisation was made ineffective. When it is also remembered that the powers of the Commissioners were those of prohibition rather than initiation, the continued defiance of the Merthyr Tydfil Board can be readily understood in the face of their appalling problems and their fears of further rebellions.

Assistant Commissioner William Day was aware in 1842 that this Board was the most difficult in his district, with many abuses prevailing there. Its methods of accounting and other irregularities came under sharp criticism; it was noted that relieving officers had given relief to paupers for a considerable amount of time in advance and that even the rents of able-bodied paupers were being paid (PRO MH12/16326, 23 May 1842). Little heed was taken of his reprimand and the Commissioner was driven to make the comment, '*They must be left to the Auditor!*'

The office of Guardian was regarded as burdensome and unpopular. Long hours were spent enquiring into the circumstances of hundreds of applicants for relief, and in the course of one meeting, there would often have to be two or three chairmen. Lady Charlotte Guest was worried when in March 1837, her husband replaced J. B. Bruce as chairman (Bessborough, 1952, p. 46). She recounted in her diary how strongly she disapproved of his accepting this office, as she believed that the strong feeling among the workers against the New Poor Law, allied with the high prices and falling wages they were experiencing, would provide political capital for her husband's opponents. She believed that while the principles of the New Poor Law were sound, '*some of the details were too bad except for slaves*'.

It was typical of the early attitude in this Union that during the election of Guardians in April, 1841, only three out of nine parishes responded, giving the Merthyr Tydfil parish a majority of 11 to 3. Fresh orders were then issued. The same thing happened in 1845 when only five out of nine parishes elected Guardians, thus making further elections necessary. Gradually, the pattern emerged of the routine, humdrum, weekly work being performed by a handful of town Guardians, many of the others attending only when an appointment of an officer was to be made, or a matter of vital importance discussed. Thus, in March 1838, for the appointment of Morgan William David (the keeper of a

Lady Charlotte Guest. Oil painting by Richard Buckner.

public house) as a relieving officer, there were 16 Guardians present, whereas *The Cardiff and Merthyr Guardian* complained that only a handful, sometimes as few as three, were usually present. Assistant Commissioner Day commented in 1842 that '*no person of education attended the Board, the Chairman himself being a tradesman*' (PRO MH12/16326, 3 Dec. 1842).

The Homeless Poor. A cartoon of 1859 from *Punch*. Its caption read 'Ah! We're badly off, but just think of the poor middle classes who are obliged to eat roast mutton and boiled fowl every day'.

Outdoor relief remained the Guardians' policy in Merthyr Tydfil from 1836 to 1853 and even that was in money not in kind. The Assistant Commissioners tried to persuade the Board of Guardians to advertise for contracts for bread and flour but received the reply that *'Merthyr Tydfil was different from agricultural districts and neighbouring manufacturing districts'* (Minutes MTBG, 25 March 1837). Unsuccessful attempts were made to advertise in *The Cambrian* and *The Bristol Mercury*, but after 1839, the idea of relief in kind was dropped.

The following extracts reflect the attitude of the Board of Guardians and Table 3 shows their increasing reliance on outdoor relief in money, not in kind, between 1837 and 1853.

> *'It was recommended by the Assistant Commissioner that a portion of relief to the poor should be given in kind, and he advised that a Contract for Bread or Flour, should be advertised for, to be delivered at three places within the Union.*
>
> *Resolved upon the motion of Morgan Morgan Esq, seconded by Mr Thomas Evans that the question respecting the contract for Bread or Flour be postponed'.* (Minutes MTBG, 12 Nov. 1836).

> *'Moved by Rowland Fothergill Esqre. seconded by W. Purnell and carried unanimously—that the following reply be forwarded to the Poor Law Commissioners.*
>
> *The Board of Guardians have hitherto refrained from relieving in kind from various reasons which appeared to them politic, considering the population of the Merthyr Union to be differently circumstanced not only from agricultural districts, but also from the manufacturing districts even in their own immediate neighbourhood.*

Merthyr Tydfil High Street in 1850. A drawing by a local artist.

It is however very far from their wish to obstruct the recommendation of the Commissioners or to thwart the Law of the Land, and they have therefore resolved to insert an advertisement for a Contract of Bread or Flour, trusting that the Commissioners will give them large discretion as the objects to which such relief in kind shall be administered'.

(Minutes MTBG, 25 March 1837).

TABLE 3

AMOUNTS PAID TO RELIEVING OFFICERS

DATE			AMOUNT
7 Jan. 1837 – 25 March 1837.	...	...	£1,308.
1 April 1837 – 17 March 1838.	...	...	£5,202 – 9 – 8.
31 March 1838 – 30 March 1839.	...	...	£5,202 – 17 – 5.
1 April 1839 – 28 March 1840.	...	...	£5,262 – 17 – 1.
4 April 1840 – 20 March 1841.	...	...	£5,957 – 2 – 0.
27 March 1841 – 26 March 1842.	...	...	£7,129 – 0 – 0.
2 April 1842 – 1 April 1843.	...	...	£9,434 – 0 – 0.
8 April 1843 – 23 March 1844.	...	...	£8,333 – 9 – 8.
30 March 1844 – 29 March 1845.	...	...	£8,703 – 0 – 0.
5 April 1845 – 28 March 1846.	...	...	£7,803 – 0 – 0.
4 April 1846 – 20 March 1847.	...	...	£8,201 – 4 – 0.
27 March 1847 – 25 March 1848.	...	...	£11,426 – 11 – 5.
1 April 1848 – 31 March 1849.	...	...	£11,400 – 0 – 0.
7 April 1849 – 30 March 1850.	...	...	£14,545 – 0 – 0.
6 April 1850 – 29 March 1851.	...	...	£14,640 – 0 – 0.
5 April 1851 – 27 March 1852.	...	...	£14,725 – 0 – 0.
3 April 1852 – 26 March 1853.	...	...	£14,035 – 0 – 0.
2 April 1853 – 25 March 1854.	...	...	£10,385 – 0 – 0.

(Figures taken from Minutes MTBG, 7 Jan. 1837 - 25 March 1854).

The sums allocated to relieving officers for disbursement during these early years show the level of expenditure during the period prior to the opening of the workhouse in 1853, though they are by no means the total expenditure. From 1834 to 1836, there was a general decrease in poor relief in Glamorgan as a whole, the cost per head being lowered from 6s.4d. to 5s.5d. per head (P. L. C. Report, 1836, pp. 564-5). In Merthyr Tydfil Union in the 1840s, the increase was due to the effects of periodic industrial recessions and to the serious consequences of sickness. Epidemics of typhus in 1847, of smallpox in 1848, and cholera in 1849, left a burden on the poor rates. The decreases during 1844, 1845 and 1846 reflect the prosperity in the iron industry brought about by the railway boom. The revival of trade in 1853 and the opening of the workhouse, account for the fall during the years 1852-4.

To sum up, the functioning of this Board in these early years reveals the attitudes of ironmasters, landowners, property owners, traders and businessmen who, as Guardians, were anxious to keep down the poor rates while ensuring that the provision of poor relief remained as flexible as possible. Their efforts to achieve these aims in an area affected by rapid social and economic change make it an interesting Union in which to examine the application of the New Poor Law.

Aberdare in the 1860s.

CHAPTER 4

The relief of the Able-bodied between 1836 and 1853

By the mid-nineteenth century, as we have already observed, Merthyr Tydfil and Aberdare were boom towns. Because of the working of the 'trade cycle', slumps succeeded booms and depressions followed expansions, which were perplexing to the Board of Guardians whose duties were to administer the Poor Law in their Union, not to understand the causes of poverty. The Poor Law Report of 1834 had recommended the refusal of outdoor relief to the able-bodied and their dependants as soon as possible after the establishment of the Unions. The Poor Law Amendment Act provided that relief to the able-bodied should be granted only according to the rules of the Commissioners. It did not define 'able-bodied persons'; they became subject to one group of regulations which allowed outdoor relief subject to certain conditions, and to a second group which forbade it, subject certain exceptions. Outdoor relief could be provided if one third or one half was in kind i.e. loaves of bread. After 1842, under the Outdoor Labour Test Order, it could be granted to able-bodied men and their dependants, provided the men did task work such as the breaking of stones. The exceptions for granting such relief arose from: sudden and urgent necessity, sickness, accident or mental infirmity, and the burial of a member of the family. Also excepted were the families of able-bodied paupers in gaol or absent in the armed forces or living outside the Union. Little attention was paid to paupers on outdoor relief and very little information is available about the conditions under which they lived.

The problem of the able-bodied became most acute during the trade recessions and strikes of the 'hungry forties', when the greatest difficulty facing the Board of Guardians was the provision of task work. The severe distress of 1842 caused by a recession in the iron industry made the provision of such work difficult.

A letter from Anthony Hill, the ironmaster, reflects this depression: '*The Clerk read a note from Mr. A. Hill . . . regretting his inability to afford employment to Herbert Williams or any other persons for whom he might apply and further stating it would be useless for the Relieving Officer to apply again*' (Minutes MTBG, 11 Dec. 1841).

Men at the Dowlais Works suffered a 10% cut in wages at the end of January 1842 and consequently many workmen and their families emigrated to America in search of better prospects (*CMG* 5 Feb. 1842). The Merthyr Tydfil

Board of Guardians found difficulty in collecting sufficient funds to meet what was estimated as a ten-fold increase in able-bodied pauperism, so the Clerk wrote to the churchwardens of Aberdare parish begging them to find employment for the large numbers receiving relief (Minutes MTBG, 26 Feb. 1842).

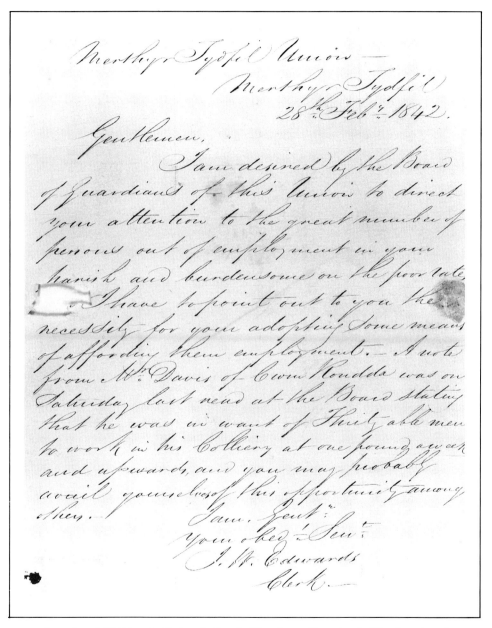

Letter from J. W. Edwards, Clerk to the Board of Guardians, addressed to the Churchwardens of Aberdare parish, 1842.

An offer of work in the Rhondda Valley was acted upon: '*Resolved that the following persons be recommended to Mr. Davis of Cwm Rhondda for employment in his colliery he having written a note stating that he is in want of Thirty Colliers at wages of one pound a week and upwards.*

    Morgan Morgan of Llanwonno Parish
    Richard Edwards   Vaynor Parish
    William Jenkins   Llanfabon Parish'.
(Minutes MTBG, 26 Feb. 1842).

Dowlais House and town, 1850.

The surveyor of parish highways was ordered to reduce the price of breaking stones from 1s.9d. to 1s.6d. per ton to be paid to labourers sent by the Guardians. This rate was reduced on 9 April, 1842, to 1s.3d. a yard, with further reductions to 1s.1d. and finally to 7d. a yard by November 1842. An offer made by the ironmaster Fothergill, at Abernant, to provide work on the roads for Aberdare paupers suspected of being unwilling to work was accepted with alacrity on 4 June 1842.

Some of the Irish-born paupers were ordered back to Ireland, though some resisted, as they were reported for running away from the constable in charge.

'*The Constable employed by the parish of Gelligaer to remove certain Irish paupers to Swansea, previously to their embarkation to Ireland, having stated that they had all left him, and refused to go, but one;—Ordered that steps be taken for apprehending them and bringing them before Magistrates*'.
(Minutes MTBG, 23 April 1842).

The real test for this Union came in February 1848, with the prospect of mass unemployment which would inevitably follow if the Dowlais Iron Company closed the Works rather than meet the vastly increased payments demanded by the Bute Estate on the renewal of the Company's lease.

The seriousness of the situation was reflected in this entry:

'The Clerk read a letter from the Poor Law Board of the 5th instant relative to the relief of able-bodied paupers when it was Resolved;

That there is every probability that within three weeks of this day some thousands of able-bodied men will be deprived of their usual means of support by the stoppage of the Dowlais Iron Works, the men having already received a month's notice to that effect, and will be unable to find immediate employment anywhere, and that in consequence of the serious and unprecedented urgency of the case the Guardians respectfully suggest that one of the Poor Law Commissioners should come down to assist the Board in their deliberations as to the course adopted.'

(Minutes MTBG, 10 Feb. 1848).

At this time, Inspector Aneurin Owen was sent down from London to assist the Guardians in the crisis. He listed the ironworks in the boundaries of the Union : (PRO MH12/16328, 12 Feb. 1848).

TABLE 4

	FURNACES
Rhymney	4
Dowlais	18
Penydarren...	6
Cyfarthfa	11
Plymouth	8
Aberdare	6
Gadlys	2
Hirwaun	4
	59

(PRO MH 12/16328, 12 Feb. 1848).

The total number of people employed at these works was 23,600, of whom 6,600 were at Dowlais which faced possible closure, and 2,000 at Penydarren, where trade was said to be very slack. Inspector Owen estimated that 8,600 people would be out of work with 21,500 dependent on them.

It is interesting to see what suggestions were made by the Inspector to provide task work for the able-bodied who applied for relief. First, he suggested that land should be acquired which able-bodied paupers could dig! Then he advised that perhaps they would be able to find jobs at the other ironworks or in the building of railways. The Guardians knew the local situation well and did not hesitate to tell him so; they felt that men who had been employed in the heat of furnaces were hardly suitable for outside work such as digging or stone-breaking because, in winter months, they would inevitably be affected by

MINERS STONE BREAKING.

A stone-breaking scene during the lock-out of 1875. *The London Illustrated News.*

illness. Secondly, they considered that if employment became available at other works elsewhere, the men would go there naturally, so that it might only be necessary to support their wives and children in their absence. The sole form of task work the Guardians would consider offering was stone-breaking, which they wanted to control themselves.

The Poor Law Board accepted the arrangements in Merthyr Tydfil Union as long as the Inspector kept them informed of what happened. The Board of Guardians then resorted to the doubtful expedient of supplementing wages with poor relief on the grounds that reducing hours in order to share out work did not enable men to earn sufficient to keep their families, and they were not prepared to make men leave work-sharing to take the Outdoor Labour Test. The Poor Law Board was reluctant to sanction such a solution but had no effective alternative to offer (PRO MH12/16328, 29 April 1848). As a further measure, it was decided that Irish applicants for relief were to be sent back to Ireland at this time.

> '*The Clerk reported that with reference to the removal of Irish paupers he had sent for the regulations of the Justices and in pursuance thereof written to the keepers of the Prisons at Cardiff and Swansea respectively for information as to vessels sailing to the specified ports.*'
> (Minutes MTBG, 26 Feb. 1848).

> '*The clerk reported that he had gone to Cardiff on Tuesday to inquire as to vessells for Ireland when he found the captains refused to take a female passenger and all the male Irish having refused to attend the Justices nothing could be done for the present.*'
> (Minutes MTBG, 26 Feb. 1848).

Fortunately, by the end of April 1848, the crisis over the renewal of the lease came to an end when an agreement was reached between the Dowlais Company and the Bute Trustees.

One of the results of this potentially overwhelming situation was the pressure put on the Board of Guardians to provide a workhouse in the Union. Inspector Farnell attended their meeting on 17 June 1848, to expound this point (PRO MH12/16328, 17 June 1848). He emphasised that in an industrial area like Merthyr Tydfil, a slump in trade would always throw large numbers of people on to the rates. For this reason, a workhouse and land on which able-bodied men could work should be acquired. It was noteworthy that of the 18 unions in South Wales, only one showed an increase in expenditure on the 1836 figures: that was Merthyr Tydfil Union where all paupers were relieved in cash and no bread was ever given.

The Chairman responded by reiterating the foolhardiness of sending men who worked in intense heat out in the open, but the Inspector dismissed the objection by saying that if they were medically unfit, they could produce certificates. The Guardians also pointed out that because of the trade recession there were thousands in Merthyr Tydfil who could not earn enough to support themselves, and that it would be futile to send thousands to a workhouse which might only accommodate 450. The Inspector emphasised that while in an

The labour yard in Bethnal Green Union, London, 1868.

emergency, outdoor relief could be given, yet a workhouse could always be used to determine who were the genuine applicants and who were the 'dangerous characters' who should be put inside. It needed stronger arguments than these to convince the Board of Guardians that they should introduce such an unpopular institution, or that they should abandon outdoor monetary relief to the able-bodied. Events overtook them in the form of serious epidemics which placed an even greater burden on the poor rates.

In 1850 *The Morning Chronicle*, the London newspaper, ran a series of long and detailed articles on 'Labour and the Poor in England and Wales'. The articles on the Iron Trades at Merthyr Tydfil and Dowlais, written between 4 March and 26 April, included the following acute observations:

'Considering that the population is almost entirely dependent upon manual labour - that employment, fluctuating with the prosperity or depression of the iron trade, is unsteady and often insufficient - and that wages have been for a long time unusually low - it is rather a matter of surprise than otherwise that pauperism is not more prevalent than I found in the mining districts of South Wales. This speaks well for the provident habits of the workman, and attests his aversion to receive parochial assistance except in the last extremity ... The 'Sick Fund' and 'Doctor's Fund' at the ironworks, with the 'Benefit Societies' which are very

numerous, have been of essential service in this particular, at once limiting the burden of the rates, and preserving the self-respect of the workman, who, but for these provisions would in cases of severe sickness or accident be reduced to the humiliating necessity of obtaining relief from the parish'.
(Ginswick, 1983, p. 80).

This viewpoint is illustrated by the suffering of the able-bodied during strikes. A bitter strike broke out in Aberdare in October 1850, over a wage-cut by the sale-coal colliery owners. In all, about 840 men and boys were thrown out of employment, with great suffering to themselves and their families. Most of them, according to *The Morning Chronicle*, lived on credit, but their subsequent privations were 'dreadful'. Evidence taken by the Correspondent from one man was very telling:

'I am a sea collier, and have worked so for twenty years. I have earned as much as 30/- a week; but the last few weeks I worked, I got no more than 7/6d a week. The works were so full of men that I could earn no more. There was little or no demand for coal ... We can't get employed anywhere hereabouts. Though I have only been three months at work in ---'s pit, I have seen in that time three boys burnt and a horse killed by firedamp. I have twice been in the fire and burnt, and have sometimes had injuries from falls of earth and stone. I lost my wife three months ago of cholera. I have five children to support, we are badly off. When I am employed, we get meat once or twice a week. I pay 7 shs. a month rent, and have my coal, as all colliers do, for nothing. Only one of my children is in school'
(Ginswick, 1983, pp. 125-6).

This sad account provides insight into the collier's precarious existence and his desperate poverty. The man was described as looking utterly dejected though his neighbour testified that he was a prudent, careful person. The neighbour, herself a widow, was also feeling the effects of the strike:

'I am a poor widow. Two years ago I had a dear boy, who helped to support me, carried home to me a corpse. He was only twenty-three years old, and was killed by firedamp in his pit. His two younger brothers are working now and support me; they are out of employ through this strike, and I don't know what will become of us', (Ginswick, 1983, pp. 125-6).

Despite such harsh poverty and cruel working conditions, the workers were prepared to withstand the effects of the strike: the Abernant colliers were out for nine weeks and the rest for three to four weeks. H. A. Bruce (son of J. B. Bruce, see biographical notes), as stipendiary magistrate, was called upon to deal with a Cwmbach collier who was charged with vagrancy - begging for bread in the streets of Aberdare. He used this opportunity to lecture the colliers on the futility of striking and exhorted them to return to work. *'Men should be taught that the price of labour, wages, did not depend on their combinations [unions], but on the state of the market'.* (*The Morning Chronicle*, p. 128). His remarks were translated into Welsh for wider publication, but were complete anathema to men who were subjected to such brutalising conditions. (See Appendix 3).

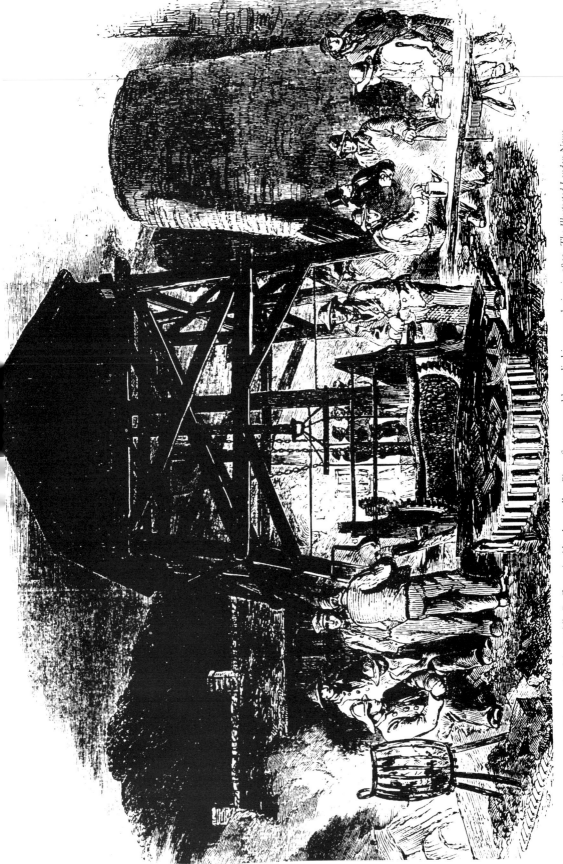

The mouth of the Middle Duffryn pit, Aberdare valley. Sixty-five men and boys died in an explosion in 1852. *The Illustrated London News.*

BURIALS in the Parish of *Aberdare*
in the County of *Glamorgan* in the Year 18*49*

Name.	Abode.	When buried.	Age.	By whom the Ceremony was performed
Rees Jenkins No. 745	Cwmbach	Aug. 12.	23 years	Henry Jones Davies
Thomas Phillips No. 746	Cwmbach	Aug. 12.	23 years	John Griffith
John Thomas No. 747	Cwmbach	Aug. 12.		John Griffith
William Thomas No. 748	Cwmbach	Aug. 12.	11 years	John Griffith
Thomas Smith No. 749	Cwmbach	Aug. 12.	11 years	John Griffith
David Davies No. 750	Cwmbach	Aug. 12.		John Griffith
David Davies Jun. No. 751	Cwmbach	Aug. 12.	14 years	John Griffith
Hugh Davies No. 752	Cwmbach	Aug. 12.		John Griffith

Eight entries relating to the victims of a colliery explosion, 1849. Aberdare parish burial register.

The Troedyrhiw colliery accident, 1877. Sketch of a scene at the pit's mouth.
The Illustrated London News

Meanwhile the strikers demonstrated on Hirwaun Common, where a crowd of 7,000 people assembled. (Parry, 1984, p. 12). Soldiers and extra policemen were drafted into the area to maintain order. 'Scotch Cattle' (bands of workmen who avenged themselves against 'non-union' men and employers, and adopted the red bull's head as their symbol), were active against 'blacklegs', one of whom was fatally wounded in 1850. The crude, raw emotions which surfaced at this time were shown by the hostility displayed at the funerals of the relatives of men who continued to work during the strike. '*They were saluted by the most heartless yells and laughter, and by the discordant sounds from beating frying pans, tin plates and kettles*' (Parry, 1984, p. 12). Despite the militancy of the colliers and the extreme deprivation they suffered, these early attempts to organise effective trade unions were difficult to sustain, yet out of the seeds of these experiences there gradually emerged the first united movement of colliers in the 1857-8 strike. The minutes of the Merthyr Tydfil Board of Guardians make no reference to the 1850 strike, so one can only speculate that this was because the able-bodied did not fall back on the poor rates, or that the Guardians were too concerned about setting up a workhouse and the effects of the cholera epidemic of 1849, to pay more attention to the situation in Aberdare parish.

VAGRANTS

In addition to those who could not obtain work, there were those determined not to do so, a large proportion of them being vagrants. As the largest industrial centre in Wales in 1834, it is understandable that Merthyr Tydfil should have had a 'floating' population. Dr. A. H. John estimated that, in 1849, between 10,000 and 11,000 vagrants circulated through the town every year. (John, 1950, p. 72). Many were undoubtedly looking for work, but some were vagrants and tramps who had no intention of supporting themselves. The policy of the New Poor Law of 1834 with regard to vagrants was to ignore them as a class and to relieve them only in the workhouse. The strict application of 'the workhouse test' was ineffective in this instance because vagrants simply regarded workhouses as lodging-houses. The Commissioners came to recognise this and between 1841 and 1844, there followed a series of regulations and suggestions designed to make a night's stay in the workhouse as unpleasant as possible for them. There was to be a separate vagrant ward without a fire: smoking and card-playing were strictly forbidden; vagrants were to be bathed, their bedding was to be inferior to that of other workhouse inmates, furthermore, they were to be prosecuted under the Vagrancy Acts.

As Merthyr Tydfil Union was without a workhouse until 1853, such measures did not apply during this early period. In fact, this Union was a centre of attraction to tramps precisely because there was no workhouse. Inspector Farnell of the Poor Law Board pointed out that as long as Merthyr Tydfil Union alone in South Wales was without a workhouse and the means of applying a labour test to vagrants, it would always be an attraction to the most disreputable characters who swarmed into the area (*CMG* 24 June 1848). Hundreds of idle, profligate vagabonds, who polluted the morals of the town

Taken by the police in a three-penny lodging house. Engraving by George Cruikshank, 1848.

and burdened the rates, gave Merthyr Tydfil a sinister reputation as a den of iniquity. He estimated that it cost 6/- a week to maintain a vagrant in a lodging-house, whereas in a workhouse the cost was only 3/2d a week. Tramps in this Union were always given money as poor relief, whereas the Inspector contended that if they were given bread, they would not be seen again.

During the bad years 1847-1849, vagrancy increased at a dangerous rate throughout the whole country. In the depression of 1848, the town of Merthyr Tydfil was inundated with beggars from all parts of the country (*CMG* 2 Dec. 1848). The Poor Law Board suggested in an official circular in July and August 1848, that a police constable who had knowledge of vagrants, and was feared by them, would be useful as an assistant to relieving officers. Merthyr Tydfil Board of Guardians followed this advice with immediate results. H. A. Bruce referred to it in a speech he made at Aberdare (*CMG* 21 July 1849). Whereas, at one time, 120-130 tramps were given relief in the town of Merthyr Tydfil every week, he said, since Superintendent Wrenn had been given responsibility for casual relief, the number of applicants had fallen to 30-40 a week. He attributed this result to the fact that they were afraid to go to the police-station to be examined.

The problem may have lessened but did not disappear, for Bruce referred to it again in a public lecture in Merthyr Tydfil in 1852 (*CMG* 7 Feb. 1852). He dealt with the widespread belief that the town was a centre of crime and depravity. It admittedly provided more than its fair share of criminals within the county during the Quarter Sessions, but if the lists of Merthyr offenders were carefully examined, it would be found that most of them were vagrants – Welsh, English and, above all, Irish, who were attracted to the town during the winter by cheap fuel which could be readily obtained even without payment. They were also influenced by the lack of a workhouse. Large numbers of tramps living by plunder were convicted annually of theft in Merthyr Tydfil and consequently increased the list of criminals from that town.

The appalling conditions in lodging-houses, where they stayed, were portrayed graphically by the Correspondent of *The Morning Chronicle* (Ginswick, 1983, pp. 89-91). He described a lodging house in Caedraw where the floor was '*broken and unwashed and the rooms stinking and filthy in the last degree*'. One room contained only a small barrel, two stools, a bench and a round table, with dirty cutlery, crockery and kettles as utensils. Beds in this lodging-house cost 2d.-4d. a night. In another lodging-house with four rooms, there were 16 people sleeping in two rooms on the ground floor alone. They slept four in a bed, two beds to a room. As the lodging-house keeper would not allow the upstairs rooms to be inspected, it could only be assumed that comparable conditions existed there. In the midst of all these people, the Correspondent saw an orphan pauper girl, four years of age, barefooted and dirty, boarded out by the Guardians of Merthyr Tydfil at 2/6d a week.

Not until the provision of a workhouse in 1853 could any attempt be made to deal with able-bodied paupers, vagrants and orphans, all of whom existed in conditions which defy description.

MERTHYR TYDFIL IN THE 1850s

Diagram showing locations within the area of the Union.
(Based on a map by Clive Thomas, published in *Merthyr Tydfil in the 1840's* by Keith Strange.)

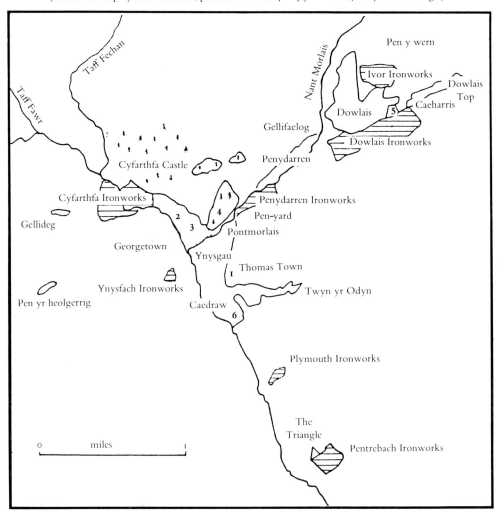

Key

1 Workhouse
2 Tydfil's Well
3 China (Pontystorehouse)
4 Penydarren House
5 Dowlais House
6 Plymouth Street

CHAPTER 5
The Sick, 1836-1853

Typhus in 1847, smallpox in 1848 and cholera in 1849 - these were the epidemics which ravaged the Merthyr Tydfil Union. It fell to the Board of Guardians, in the absence of appropriate local government machinery, to assume responsibility when such crises occurred. The Poor Law Amendment Act of 1834 had not laid down policy regarding sick paupers who were allowed to receive medical attendance in their own homes. They were excepted from the Outdoor Labour Test Order of 1842, outdoor relief being given even if the head of the family was earning wages. The Poor Law Commissioners were very much concerned with the organisation of medical attendance, the area of each medical officer's district, the method of selecting him and the number of cases he attended. The three medical officers' districts set up in Merthyr Tydfil Union in 1836 were considered by the Commissioners to be too large. The Board of Guardians disagreed and threatened that if more medical officers were engaged, the salaries of the existing ones would be cut down to pay for them. When residents in Gelligaer parish complained of the inconvenience of their medical officer living so far away, the Poor Law Commissioners intervened to ask the Board of Guardians to make a rearrangement (PRO MH12/16327, 1 March 1845). The outcome was that Dr. Redwood of Rhymney was appointed as medical officer for Brithdir in the parish of Gelligaer at a salary of £10 per annum, while a proportionate decrease was made in the salary of Dr. Davies, medical officer of Gelligaer. Dr. Redwood was further required to be the vaccination officer in his area.

The Vaccination Act of 1840 provided that vaccination against smallpox could be given at public expense and should be administered by the Boards of Guardians. In Merthyr Tydfil Union, the boundaries of the medical officers' Vaccination Districts coincided with Registration Districts and it was observed that the numbers vaccinated were less than half of those registered at birth. This led the medical officers to the conclusion that compulsory vaccination was the only remedy, for it was obvious that parents of young children showed great indifference to having their children vaccinated (PRO MH12/16327, 13 Aug. 1845).

The Nuisances Removal Act of 1848 concentrated the power and responsibility for the removal of offensive and dangerous materials in the hands of the Union medical officers. During epidemics, all places certified by them as being a danger to health were to be cleansed every 24 hours. They were to inspect lodging-houses and make landlords ensure that they were properly ventilated. Dispensaries were to be opened to supply medicines and advice, and 'houses of refuge' were to be provided to which endangered families might be sent. An Order in Council put the Act into force on the approach of an epidemic. It was an unsatisfactory measure mainly because it proved to be impossible to get Boards of Guardians to take their public health responsibilities seriously. They saw their prime duty as the administration of poor relief, with health matters coming as a poor second. Not until the passing of the Public Health Acts of 1848, 1866 and 1875 could these matters be dealt with more effectively.

In 1847, typhus was reported in various parts of Merthyr Tydfil. The chief areas affected were the crowded and filthy parts of the town where the poorest people lived. Many of them were Irish families, driven out of their farms and homesteads by the Great Famine of 1846, who had arrived in Merthyr in search of work. Typhus fever was a disease of dirt, and the organism which caused it was carried by lice which infested unwashed bodies and the seams of dirty clothing. This is why it was referred to as 'gaol fever', from its prevalence wherever many people were herded closely together, wearing the same clothes for prolonged periods and lacking the means of ensuring bodily cleanliness. It was endemic in Merthyr Tydfil, one death in nine being caused by it during the period 1840-1845.

The slums of Merthyr Tydfil were as bad as the worst living conditions anywhere in the whole of Britain. *The Morning Chronicle* Correspondent described the notorious conditions in the cellars of 'China':

Interior of a collier's cottage. *The Illustrated London News*, 1873.

'*There is a quarter of the town extending along a flat on the right-hand bank of the Taff, from the lowest point of High Street, towards Cyfarthfa - the proper name of which is Pont-y-Storehouse, but like the unhappy and lawless people who inhabit it, the place has an alias and is generally known by the name of 'China'. The houses are mere huts of stone - low, confined, ill-lighted and unventilated; they are built without pretensions to regularity, and form a maze of courts and tortuous lanes, hardly passable in many places for house refuse, rubbish and filth. In some parts, they are considerably below the level of the road and descent is by ladders. Such houses are called 'the cellars'. Here it is that, in a congenial atmosphere, the crime, disease and penury of Merthyr are for the most part located. Thieves, prostitutes, vagrants, the idle, the reckless, the dissolute, here live in miserable companionship. This neighbourhood formed the main scene of our inquiries; and what I saw that day of misery, degradation and suffering, I shall remember to the end of my life*'.
(Ginswick, 1983, pp. 86–87).

The conditions under which the poorest people lived in Merthyr Tydfil in 1847 were also outlined in an article in the local press (*CMG* 3 April 1847). It stated that the accumulation of filth in certain localities was utterly disgusting

A court for King Cholera. Drawing by John Leech in *Punch*, 1852.

45

and the habits of the people were devoid of all sense of decency. The badly-ventilated lodging-houses of Ynysgau and Pont-y-Storehouse (China) were crowded with destitute people who day after day dunned the relieving officers and besieged the Board of Guardians on Saturdays for poor relief. It was a desperate situation over which the poor and the sick themselves had no control since they were the victims of extreme poverty and of a total lack of public health provision in the town. As T. W. Rammell stated in 1850, 'For all intents and purposes of civic government, Merthyr Tydfil is as destitute as the smallest rural village in the empire' (Rammell, 1850, p. 12). Under these conditions, it made little sense for one of the inspectors in *The Report of the Commission on Education, 1847*, to castigate people in the 'iron districts' as being 'essentially animal in their habits'.

Poor Law and Public Health were two sides of the same coin: poverty produced sickness and sick people became paupers, the two problems were one and indivisible. The typhus epidemic was such as to compel the Guardians to look for accommodation for sick paupers and they resolved in April 1847 to negotiate for the Old Brewery. In the event, it was decided that the premises were unsuitable, despite the total lack of hospital accommodation or of a refuge for relations of those affected by epidemics.

These decisions appear in the following entries:

'*Asylum Special Meeting. Moved by Mr. J. C. Wolrige   Seconded by Mr. G. Martin and Resolved*

That it is expedient and imperative to provide an asylum for the sick and destitute at this period of sickness and distress, and that a place be immediately provided and that Mr. Lewis Lewis the Vice chairman be requested to negotiate for the Old Brewery for that purpose and that a Special Meeting be called next Saturday to receive Mr. Lewis's Report.'
(Minutes MTBG, 17 April 1847).

'*Mr. Lewis the Vice Chairman reported that the Old Brewery might be had for £40 per ann. if repaired by Landlord or £35 if by tenant.*

Proposed by Mr. John Evans and seconded by Mr. Martin that it is not expedient at the present time to rent the Old Brewery for the purpose of converting it into a Fever Hospital for the use of the parish of Merthyr.

Carried unanimously with the exception of Mr. Lewis Lewis and Mr. Wolridge.'
(Minutes MTBG, 24 April 1847).

The extreme distress in Merthyr Tydfil at this time caused T. J. Dyke, a local doctor destined to become its first medical officer of health, to write to the Board of Guardians. Born in Merthyr Tydfil in 1816, Dr. T. J. Dyke was a highly respected medical practitioner who had served an apprenticeship to surgeons at the Cyfarthfa Works prior to studying medicine in London where he qualified as a member of the Royal College of Surgeons. He returned to Merthyr in 1839 and became a parish surgeon and surgeon to the Dowlais Iron Company. He was appointed as medical officer to Merthyr Tydfil Local Board of Health in 1863, in which capacity he produced a series of annual reports which provided important information about public health conditions. He has been described as 'an invaluable public servant' who provided the leadership, professionalism and commitment which led to the eventual solution of the enormous public health problems which existed in Merthyr Tydfil. He remained in office until his death in 1900 and stands out as a dedicated and compassionate humanitarian.

In May 1847, Dr. Dyke wrote to the Board of Guardians to complain about the suffering of sick paupers (PRO MH12/16328, 14 May 1847). He cited the case of Josiah Robins, a ragman, who lived in two cellars under a row of houses.

Dr. T. J. Dyke.
An oil painting which hangs in the Aberdare Masonic Temple.

These two rooms were ten feet square, had floors made partly of earth and partly of pitch, with one window and one fireplace. The bedding consisted of two straw beds and heaps of straw. Both rooms were damp and the bed-clothes were filthy. In all, 13 people occupied these two rooms, one of whom was a young woman whom Robins took in as a lodger. She contracted typhus and died. In quick succession, Robins and the other occupants of these cellars caught

Workers' houses in West Lane, Georgetown, Merthyr Tydfil.

the disease. Dr. Dyke pointed out that, even though the parish medical officer had attended them, poor relief alone was of little use in preventing the spread of disease. He was strongly of the opinion that they should have been removed from this 'noisome den' and put in a place more suitable for human habitation. He wanted these cellars to be closed, for each successive batch of inhabitants would inevitably be affected by the fever, and the Guardians would be responsible for maintaining them when they were alive and burying them when they were dead.

These urgent representations produced the following tardy response:

> '*The Clerk reported that he had procured the certificate of two surgeons as to the state of the Room written about by Mr. Dyke and that he was informed by the owner of the Room last evening that he had caused it to be well whitewashed.*' (Minutes MTBG, 29 May 1847).

Nor did appeals of this kind move the Poor Law Commissioners who could only suggest the requisition of tenements in which to house sick paupers. They were more concerned about the lack of a workhouse than with the provision of separate hospital facilities, urging that a properly-equipped workhouse would be the best way to meet such emergencies. As for the cellars, individual Guardians were advised to use their influence in order to persuade the landlord to close them (PRO MH12/16328, 31 May 1847).

As the epidemic worsened, *The Cardiff and Merthyr Guardian* reported that the sanitary condition of Merthyr Tydfil was deteriorating daily, with typhus spreading death far and wide (22 May 1847). The lodging-houses where vagrants were accommodated were a cause of great concern because they were breeding-places of the disease. It was not uncommon to find six or seven emaciated creatures huddled in cellars too small and too dirty to accommodate even one. It was believed that the fever spread from these pest holes to more open areas. Though no statistics are available relating to this epidemic, the number of deaths was said to be very great. Yet the Board of Guardians made no attempt to provide a hospital and certainly took no action with regard to a workhouse, mainly because public opinion was too strongly opposed to it and they were afraid of popular resistance at a time when Chartism was again active.

The *Cardiff and Merthyr Guardian* summed up the position with regard both to a hospital and a workhouse:

'*HEALTH OF TOWNS. - However our medical men may differ as to the name by which the disease is to be distinguished which destroys the population, it is very evident that the number of deaths is very great. Of this the immense number of persons in mourning on Sunday last, who made the place appear sepulchral, and sent an involuntary shudder through our nervous system, is an abundant and convincing proof. Scurvy prevails to a very great extent, and particularly in the upper districts; and it would be well that some salutary precautions were pointed out by our medical gentlemen to prevent its rapid spread among the impoverished population. The propriety of having an airy and convenient place to locate fevered patients having been suggested to the board of guardians by Mr T J Dyke, a correspondence has taken place between the board and the Poor Law Commissioners upon the subject. With some of the suggestions of the commissioners we entirely concur, and particularly with that part of their reply which refers to the matter now under notice; but the second paragraph is not likely to be quite so palatable, for public opinion is at present too strongly opposed, however wise and convenient the establishment of a workhouse may be. The important question now is with regard to a parish hospital. We hope to see the time when Merthyr will have an infirmary; but at the present juncture, a temporary hospital appears very desirable. The guardians have as yet done nothing; what they ought to do, let our readers judge*'.
(*CMG* 12 June 1847).

Then, in February 1848, smallpox made its appearance. This was one of the 'zymotic' diseases which were common where people were crowded together. It was highly contagious and was readily transferred from one person to another. By the eighteenth century, smallpox was the most lethal illness of the very young. It became endemic in Europe, causing a number of deaths every year and flaring into great epidemics at all too frequent intervals. Though primarily a disease of childhood, persons of all ages could be infected and this was why vaccination was so important.

The Central Authority was aware of the dangerous situation in the Merthyr Tydfil Union but little or no remedial action was taken: '*The Clerk read a letter from the Poor Law Board drawing the attention of the guardians to the great prevalance of small pox in the Merthyr and Aberdare Districts as appears by the Registrar General's Report for the quarter and when the clerk was directed to cause the large Bills to be posted*' (Minutes MTBG, 26 Feb. 1848).

The overcrowded, insanitary conditions in Merthyr Tydfil lodging-houses made them perfect breeding-grounds for this dangerous fever. A member of the Board of Guardians recounted a visit he had made to a lodging-house containing sick paupers and described the gruesome conditions under which they fought for survival (*CMG* 24 June 1848). The Guardian, Lewis Lewis, went upstairs at midnight and saw seven beds in one room with two men in each bed—14 in one small loft with no ventilation. He went downstairs where he saw three beds in a room, each containing two people, and alongside a coffin containing a corpse. He bitingly remarked that this was the way that parochial relief was doled out in the parish of Merthyr Tydfil. For these reasons, he and D. W. James were prepared to second H. A. Bruce's proposition on 17 June 1848, '*That the interests of humanity and economy would be equally promoted by the erection of a workhouse*'. (See Chapter 7).

The mortality tables for these years reveal an appalling state of affairs. Though the toll of the 1848 smallpox epidemic is not shown, the effects of such illnesses on infant mortality were sensational.

TABLE 5

BIRTHS AND DEATHS IN 7 YEARS BETWEEN 1841 AND 1847 IN THE PARISH OF MERTHYR TYDFIL

YEARS	BIRTHS	DEATHS						
		Under 1 yr.	Under 3 yrs.	Under 5 yrs.	Under 20 yrs.	TOTAL Under 20	TOTAL Above 20	TOTAL
1841	1,483	247	253	54	86	640	334	974
1842	1,531	228	160	36	68	492	289	781
1843	1,574	226	140	37	91	494	316	810
1844	1,600	360	382	135	143	1,020	497	1,517
1845	1,694	309	216	65	130	720	362	1,082
1846	1,813	335	243	62	103	743	438	1,181
1847	1,759	385	310	93	139	927	507	1,434
TOTAL	11,454	2,090	1,704	482	760	5,036	2,743	7,779
Average per yr.	1,636	299	243	69	109	719	392	1,111

(*Report to the General Board of Health on a Preliminary Inquiry into the Sewerage, Drainage and Supply of Water and the Sanitary Condition of the Inhabitants of Merthyr Tydfil . . .*, by T. W. Rammell, Esq., 1850, p. 12). [These figures were rounded by Rammell].

It is remarkable that, while the number of births during the seven years was 11,454, the deaths numbered 7,779, leaving 3,675 towards increasing the population. In that period, the population actually increased by 10,000, of which 6,400 must have resulted from immigration. During the years 1831-1841, the total increase averaged 1,518 per annum, while the excess of births over deaths was at a rate of 522 per annum. Over a fifth of the total mortality was caused by epidemics and contagious diseases. In fact, the mortality rate for Merthyr Tydfil was 33 per 1,000 which was well in excess of the average and ranked next to Manchester and Liverpool as the highest death rates in the kingdom.

Inspector Rammell pointed out that from this table it was possible to glean 'the astounding and perhaps unparalleled fact that of the 1,111 deaths per year between 1841-1847, 542 or nearly one-half were those of children under 3 years; 719 or nearly two-thirds were of people under 20 years; 299 or just over one-sixth died before the end of the first year; 542 or just under one-third died before they were 3 years of age'. He explained that such high infant mortality was in no way due to causes over which people themselves had control, and that no mothers looked after their babies better than the Welsh. The cause of this tragic situation lay in the filthy surroundings in which the children grew up. In the same report, Dr. T. J. Dyke quoted the evidence of Sir Henry De la Beche in 1845 that the average duration of life in Merthyr Tydfil among the lower classes was $17\frac{1}{2}$ years, owing to the high mortality rate of children under five years of age.

Infant mortality within a family as illustrated by an entry from the reference book
to the St. John's Aberdare churchyard plan.

The parish of Aberdare also presented a depressing picture, when Inspector Rammell took evidence there in 1853.

TABLE 6

BIRTHS AND DEATHS IN THE PARISH OF ABERDARE, BETWEEN 1846 AND 1852

BIRTHS		DEATHS					
YEARS	BIRTHS	Under 5 yrs.	5–10 yrs.	10–20 yrs.	Over 20 yrs.	TOTAL	Deaths from Epidemic, Endemic & Contagious Diseases.
1846	342	105	10	7	90	212	27
1847	351	126	9	17	106	258	70
1848	452	119	7	16	107	249	57
1849	493	171	28	43	258	500	202
1850	567	142	15	19	135	311	78
1851	594	212	15	49	141	417	110
1852	756	293	24	65	212	594	215
TOTAL	3,555	1,168	108	216	1,049	2,541	759
Average per yr.	508	167	15	31	150	363	108

(Preliminary Inquiry into the Sewerage, Drainage and Supply of Water and the Sanitary Condition of the Inhabitants of the Parish of Aberdare in the County of Glamorgan, by T. W. Rammell, Esq., 1853, p. 18).

The population in 1841 was 6,471 which by 1851 had increased to 14,999, and in 1853 stood at 16,000. Here the gross mortality was 28 in 1,000. Of the 363 deaths per year between 1846 and 1852, 167 or nearly one-half were deaths of children under 5 years; 213 or nearly two-thirds were of people under 20 years. The proportion of deaths from epidemic and contagious diseases was always high, 108 out of 363, or nearly one-third, and during 1849, the year of the cholera epidemic, it reached two-fifths. In his evidence to Inspector Rammell, one of the parish doctors stated *'Fevers principally prevail. We are never without 8 or 9 cases on hand. The population is increasing fast, and the number of cases with it. The town is very badly drained and I find most diseases in the most filthy localities'*.

The conditions giving rise to disease in Aberdare were described by Inspector Rammell, who referred to the fact that there were hundreds of houses in the town with no drainage whatsoever, the inhabitants having to throw all their filth and refuse into the streets, except in places with cesspits (which were often overflowing). In some cases, the privies were arranged so that they emptied into an open ditch, the stench from which in the summer was most offensive. One witness stated, *'In summer, the stink was so bad here that people could hardly walk by on the public footpath which leads to the parish church'*.

BURIALS in the Parish of _Aberdare_

in the County of _Glamorgan_ in the Year 18_49_

Name.	Abode.	When buried.	Age.	By whom the Ceremony was performed.
Gwenllian Howells No. 777	Village	Aug. 8.	9 years	
Henry Jones No. 778	Watchmaker's Row	August 9th	77 years	Henry Jones Davies
Margaret Morley No. 779	Mary doe	August 19th	67 years	Henry Jones
David Morgan No. 780	Village	August 20th	58 years	Henry Jones Davies
William Jeremy No. 781	Village	August 20th	4 years	Henry Jones Davies
Edward Davis No. 782	Village	August 20th	3 Months	Henry Jones Davies
William Thomas No. 783	Mountain Ash.	Aug. 21.	37 years.	John Griffith
Thomas Morley No. 784	Marsydoe	Aug. 21.	68 years	John Griffith

Cholera victims, 1849. Aberdare parish burial register.

Merthyr Tydfil's reputation as having 'a higher mortality rate than any other commercial or manufacturing town in the kingdom' was certainly unenviable, (Rammell, p. 24). Superintendent Wrenn of the police stated that he had seen Liverpool, Swansea, Bristol, Birmingham, Bath, Gloucester, Dublin and other towns, but that Merthyr Tydfil was worse than any of them. He made the pertinent observation: '*All these towns have local Acts but Merthyr has none, and I attribute the difference to this cause*'. The Clerk to the Board of Guardians stated that though, by virtue of their powers under the Nuisance Removal Act 1846, they had appointed an Inspector of Nuisances and had served notices on offenders, it was nevertheless ineffective in Merthyr Tydfil. Dung heaps existed throughout the town, and the two sewers which existed discharged into the River Taff.

Asiatic cholera, therefore, had fertile breeding ground when it appeared in these towns in 1849. Wherever people shared a common water supply and had no sanitary arrangements, there was a great risk of a water-borne disease such as cholera, more especially in high densities of population. Unfortunately, it took many years for doctors to establish the link between contaminated water and the spread of the disease. Cholera's symptoms were violent, intractable diarrhoea and vomiting, followed by a state of collapse and early death.

The following entry in the Minutes of Merthyr Tydfil Board of Guardians reflects not only their real concern about the onset of this epidemic but their state of ignorance about the disease.

'*At a Meeting of the Sanitary Committee of the Guardians for the Merthyr district . . . the Committee were attended by the Medical Gentlemen of the parish of Merthyr and by several of the principal inhabitants. Mr. Job James the Medical Officer of the Union certified that Asiatic Cholera had reached the District and that several deaths had ensued.*

Mr. Wrenn, Supt. of Police, was requested and undertook to superintend the distributing of lime all over the town of Merthyr and white liming where necessary and the clerk was directed to give orders for any materials required and that paupers be placed under Mr. Wrenn's directions . . . The Clerk was also directed to print and distribute the following Notice of the Medical Men.
                              "Public Notice
Some persons having died from Malignant Cholera within the last week we the undersigned Surgeons practising in Merthyr deem it our duty to advise the public of our opinion on the subject. Cholera is not contagious. Therefore any one may attend to the sick without fear of catching the disease.

As Cholera mostly occurs in places where there is much filth, so, to cleanse and whitewash inside and outside of houses are means well calculated to prevent the extension of the disease.'
(Minutes MTBG, 29 May 1849)

A public notice printed in the *Cardiff and Merthyr Guardian* underlined the stage of ignorance which prevailed:

'*And as there have occurred several deaths among washerwomen, the following notice is highly important:—*

CHOLERA.—NOTICE.—It is the OPINION OF MEDICAL MEN that there is LESS DANGER IN WASHING IN COLD WATER THAN IN HOT, the clothes, bed-linen, &c., which have been used by persons while they were ill, and who have died of cholera. The Cholera Committee, therefore, beg to urge on all parties the great desirability of washing all such things in COLD WATER.—By order of the Committee.—Merthyr Tydfil, July 3rd, 1849.'
(*CMG* 7 July 1849)

Over a space of four months, tragedy occurred on a massive scale and '*men died like rotten sheep*' (*The Morning Chronicle*, p. 63). To deal with the emergency, special meetings of the Board of Guardians were held almost daily. On the suggestion of Sir John Guest, they consulted a doctor sent down by the General Board of Health (PRO MH12/16328, 13 June 1849). This adviser, Dr. Sutherland, pointed out that, geographically, Merthyr Tydfil was not an unhealthy town, but in respect of sanitary matters, its condition was deplorable. It had no drainage, no water supply, no water closets, no cleansing facilities. The river running through the town was like a common sewer. Attempting to trace the cause of the epidemic, he made the observation: '*So far as I have yet ascertained, the main things which appear to have fixed the epidemic influence on particular localities are dampness, want of ventilation in the houses, and perhaps the quality of the water which is far from good*'. This last comment was nearer to the truth than he realised.

Queuing for water at a street tap, Bethnal Green, London.

Dr. Sutherland then set about helping the Board of Guardians to organise relief for the sick, (*CMG* 16 June 1849). The town was divided into nine districts, each with a Medical Officer in charge who was assisted by day visitors. Arrangements were made for the prompt reporting of all cholera cases, and for co-operating with the iron companies and the Guardians. Dispensaries were opened providing medicines day and night, and supplies were left with the managers of the various works. As far as accommodation for the sick was concerned, the Union of Merthyr Tydfil was expected to provide a house of refuge for the poor and the managers of the ironworks were to provide a wooden building for their employees. The Dowlais Company was complimented on organising 30 districts with 35 visitors; the Plymouth and Cyfarthfa Companies took similar steps, but the Penydarren Company did little towards arresting the course of the epidemic.

In Aberdare, a Sanitary Committee set up under the chairmanship of H. A. Bruce made the following arrangements:

'*It was resolved That Mr. John Smith, the Revd. John Griffith and Mr. Evan Evans be appointed a Sub-Committee to provide when occasion shall arise the necessary accommodation for persons removed from Sick houses in a shed, the use of which has been granted to the Parish by the Taff Vale Company.*

That Mr. Morgan of Abercwmboy, the Revd. Mr. David and Mr. Williams of Ynyscynon be appointed a Sub-Committee to carry out the same object at Aberamman and Abergwawr at the Old Plough Tavern, the use of which has been granted by Mr. Roberts.

That there be a Meeting of the Sanitary Committee, Guardians and other Inhabitants held at the Porch of the Church every Monday and Thursday at 3 o'clock during the prevalence of the Cholera. That Mr. Supt. Wrenn be

Entries made during the cholera epidemic of 1849, signed by Henry A. Bruce as Chairman.

authorized to purchase 12 brushes and handles for the purposes of whitewashing and to provide lime for necessary purposes'.
(Minutes MTBG, 19 June 1849).

'Ordered that Walter Walters be appointed to the charge of the House of Refuge at Gadlys upon terms of remuneration to be again fixed upon'.
(Minutes MTBG, 12 July 1849).

In Merthyr Tydfil, efforts were made to clean the town and relieve the sick (*CMG* 23 June 1849). Lime was distributed for white-washing and 'a monster dung-hill' near Bryant's Field was removed at the expense of the parish to fertilise Penydarren Park. This particular nuisance had been the source of many cholera deaths. A house of refuge was completed and a large number of people were ordered into it, most of them Irish. There was considerable prejudice towards them at this time because they were regarded as being dirty, lazy and lacking initiative. (See Appendix 4). A committee of Guardians sat daily in Dowlais and Roger Williams, the Relieving Officer was given an assistant.

'Resolved That during the present state of distress in Dowlais and the adjoining district Mr. Roger Williams be requested to reside in Dowlais for the purpose of immediately investigating all applications for relief and giving such relief as may appear necessary and that a Committee of the Guardians sit daily at the Dowlais School Room to assist him and that a report of all cases relieved be made to the Board at its usual weekly sitting for the purpose of being examined and if approved of sanctioned by the Board.'
(Minutes MTBG, 4 Aug. 1849).

Lady Charlotte Guest, writing in her diary on 31 July 1849, stated '*I am sorry to say the accounts of the cholera at Dowlais are fearfully bad. They are beyond anything I could have imagined, sometimes upward of 20 people dying in one day, and eight men constantly employed in making coffins . . . One of our medical assistants sent down from London is dying and the whole place seems in a most lamentable state. I am greatly grieved for the condition of my poor home*'. (Bessborough, 1952, p. 230).

During this critical period, little help was received by the Board of Guardians from the Poor Law Board, though a letter outlining administrative procedure was sent by the General Board of Health on 6 August 1849. Signed by Ashley, Chadwick and Southwood Smith, it gave general instructions and regulations, most of which were already being followed by the Board of Guardians. Mercifully, by 18 August 1849, there were signs of a decrease in mortality, whereupon Inspector Hurst of the Poor Law Board commended the Guardians 'for having taken every precaution' to meet the emergency.

A very different picture was painted by Inspector Robert Bowie of the General Board of Health when he visited Merthyr Tydfil in August 1849. In his view, the main causes of disease would always exist until the Public Health Act of 1848 was put into operation (PRO MH12/16328 16 Aug. 1849). Some of the evidence he cited was most graphic. For example, in one miserable, unventilated attic, he had found four severe cases of cholera. They were covered with dirty clothing and the walls of the room were being white-washed while the victims were in bed. In a room below, a girl was passing into a state of collapse while a woman and a boy were busy with pails and a brush white-washing the walls. So offensive was the smell that he ordered a man to make a hole in the roof to insert some perforated tiles. He then made the damning statement that this house was a pauper lodging-house, there being no other place to receive the sick and destitute.

Robert Bowie conveyed his strong disapproval of such conditions to the Clerk to the Board of Guardians who replied that they were grateful not only to the landlady, but to anyone else who would take in their sick poor. Inspector Bowie then sent the police to the house to remove every person except those confined to bed, and one or two attendants. He condemned some of the parish officers for their incompetence: one of the Relieving Officers had laughed at a sick pauper called Mary McCarthy when she took a medical order to him, and only under pressure did he give way to orders from Robert Bowie himself. Gradually, the mortality rate fell until, by 15 September, 1849, it was severe in one locality only—Tydfil's Well. Its persistence there could only be explained by one cause, a huge trench into which all the filth and refuse of the locality had been poured for a quarter of a century. By 22 September, as a result of decreasing numbers of cholera cases, the carting of ashes and filth, house to house visitations and the cleansing of all areas were discontinued. The final death toll was:

TABLE 7

CHOLERA AT MERTHYR-TYDFIL.

RETURN OF CASES,
Saturday, September 22, 1849.

MERTHYR.	ATTACKED.	DEAD.
Total from commencement (May 25th), as per last Report, corrected by Registration Returns up to 10 A. M., Yesterday	1779	745
New Cases, up to 10 A. M., To-day	1	1
PENYDARRAN.		
Total from commencement (June 5th), up to 10 A.M., Yesterday	272	170
New Cases, up to 10 A. M., To-day	0	0
DOWLAIS.		
Total from commencement (June 10th), up to 10 A. M., Yesterday	1196	499
New Cases, up to 10 A. M., To-day	0	1
ABERDARE.		
Total from commencement (June 24th), up to 10 A. M., Yesterday	364	104
New Cases, up to 10 A. M., To-day	0	0
TOTAL	3612	1520

FRANK JAMES,
Clerk to the Guardians.

Frank James, Clerk to the Board of Guardians, supplied Inspector Rammell with details of the increased expenditure caused in the parish of Merthyr Tydfil by the cholera epidemic of 1849:

TABLE 8

	£	s.	d.	£	s.	d.
Excess of Expenditure in Out-Relief over the former year				3,255.	2.	7.
Extraordinary Expenditure:						
Erecting, Furnishing and maintaining of House of Refuge.	217.	0.	10.			
Daily Visitors	143.	12.	0.			
Surgeons' Bills - extra medical aid	733.	8.	6.			
Medicines not included in above	20.	17.	4.			
Lime-whiting and cleansing	345.	16.	11.			
				1,460.	15.	7.
Total increased expenditure, 1849, on account of Cholera				4,715.	18.	2.

(Rammell, 1850, pp. 66-67).

In the parish of Aberdare, a comparison of the amounts of money paid by the Guardians to the three Relieving Officers during the second quarter of 1849, with the corresponding quarter of the previous year, gives some indication of the increased burden on the poor rates by the epidemic, though it was only part of the whole cost.

TABLE 9

	£	s.	d.
Amount paid to the Relieving Officers for the second quarter of 1848	3,035.	0.	0.
Amount paid to the Relieving Officers for the second quarter of 1849	4,785.	0.	0.
Increased Expenditure	1,750.	0.	0.

(Figures extracted from Minutes MTBG, July 1848 - Sep. 1849).

This amounted to an increase of over 50% in Relieving Officers' expenses in Aberdare parish in 1849 due to cholera.

Inspector Rammell pointed out that the disease left a permanent increase in expenditure in Merthyr Tydfil parish of more than £2,500 p.a. He emphasised that this provided strong evidence of the false economy of neglecting proper sanitary arrangements and that this figure was but a fraction of the actual cost of preventable disease in Merthyr Tydfil. (Rammell, 1850, p. 65). These major epidemics had the effect of making sanitary reform and the provision of a workhouse imperative in this disease-ridden Union.

Aberdare, from Abernant, in the 1860s.

CHAPTER 6

Pauper Children, 1836 - 1853

Readers of *Oliver Twist* will recall Dickens's depiction of the sufferings of pauper children. Much of what he described was replicated in Merthyr Tydfil. In 1836, the number of children in the charge of the Union was:

TABLE 10

PARISH	CHILDREN
Merthyr Tydfil	207 (including 28 bastards)
Gelligaer	23
Llanwonno	6
Llanfabon	—
Penderyn	53
Vaynor	35
Ystradyfodwg	15
Rhigos	12
Aberdare	10
TOTAL	361

(PRO MH12/16326, 4 Nov. 1836).

Children constituted 30% of the total number of paupers in the Union. By August 1849, their numbers had increased to 772, of whom 101 were orphans and 671 were the children of widows (*CMG* 4 Aug. 1849). Whatever outdoor relief was given to children, the policy of both the Poor Law Commissioners and the Board of Guardians was one of absolute non-intervention: they were not concerned about their education or welfare. Initially, Boards of Guardians were not even allowed to add twopence a week as payment for the education of a child. By 1855, this was modified so that children on outdoor relief between the ages of four and sixteen could be given education if the Guardians wished.

The Poor Law Report of 1834 had been emphatic and clear that when children entered a workhouse, they should be accommodated in a separate building under a separate staff. This was disregarded by the Poor Law Commissioners who adopted a policy of one common workhouse for each union, under a single head, with the same discipline for all classes. In the workhouse, children were classified according to age, sex and health. After 1847, the Poor Law Board took the view that this system simply manufactured paupers and wanted the children put in separate schools where they could learn trades.

Such 'progressive' ideas were anathema to Merthyr Tydfil's Guardians who showed no awareness between 1836 and 1847 of the desperate plight of orphans, illegitimate and deserted children. The one concern of the Board of Guardians was to keep down the poor rates. Even after the provision of a workhouse in 1853, the children remained there, for the Guardians were prepared to pay only lip-service to the expensive provision of a separate school.

By 1847, the condition of orphan pauper children in the Union was becoming a scandal. They were farmed out in Merthyr Tydfil parish to people of the worst possible reputation and were brought up in 'that den of infamy, the notorious cellars'. Their condition was exposed by the Correspondent of *The Morning Chronicle* who wrote:

'Wishing to satisfy myself of the authenticity of certain statements I had heard, that the pauper children in Merthyr were confided to the care of the low Irish and others living in the worst quarters of the town, and being desirous to examine into the condition of the poor in their own homes, I set apart a day to do this duty. I was accompanied by the Rector of the parish, the Rev. Mr. Campbell, who kindly undertook to be my guide. We called in the first instance at the offices of the 'Union', where we obtained the addresses of a number of illegitimate and orphan children farmed out by the parish, after which we commenced our round of inspection' (Ginswick, 1983, p. 86).

These letters were written between the 4 March and 26 April 1850, and provide the detailed descriptions which are lacking in the more formal and 'discreet' minutes of the Board of Guardians. They coincided with the campaign being waged by H. A. Bruce, stipendiary magistrate, landowner, and ex-officio member of the Board of Guardians, for the setting up of an industrial school for pauper children. J. C. Campbell, the rector of Merthyr Tydfil, was Bruce's brother-in-law and was in the forefront of the campaign to improve the treatment of these children. The Correspondent states:

'We called at the dwelling of an Irishwoman named W---, where were placed by the parish two orphan children, whose parents had lately died of cholera. An old table, two chairs, and a stool formed the only furniture of the main room of this house. The woman was out, and we found four children squatted around a handful of fire which was burning in the grate. The oldest of them might be about nine years of age. There was no fender to protect them from the fire, nor was there anyone in charge of them. The house was filthy and stinking; the floor which was strewed with the sweepings of coal, had not been washed, I should say, for weeks; the window was in several places broken, and the holes unstopped. The eldest girl had a look of intelligence. I judged her to be about nine years old. Like the others, she was barefooted, in rags; her hair was matted, and her hands, face and neck were black with dirt. She answered me as follows:

"My name is Biddy N---. I and my sister are put here by the parish. My mother and father are dead. I can't tell what my age is. I cannot read for I was never at school. I sleep with three or four other children in the room".
She pointed to an adjoining room which I entered. The only furniture it contained was a bed of straw. Here, without sheets or blankets, and with only a filthy

'Poor Jo', a photograph by O. G. Rejlander who was active in the 1860s making photographs of the poor and destitute. Although his pictures were 'staged' and sentimentalised, his work did much to raise public awareness of the plight of the poor.

counterpane to cover them, these children passed the bitterly cold nights of winter. I thought of the high mortality of infant life in Merthyr, and it seemed to me a mercy rather than otherwise, that children should be taken away from such hardships, neglect and sufferings' (Ginswick, 1983, pp. 86, 87).

'Cold, Misery and Want destroy their youngest child: they console themselves with the Bottle'.
Illustration by George Cruikshank, 1847.

They called on another house where pauper children were boarded out and the first thing they saw on entering was

'the corpse of a child in a winding sheet, laid upon a table; a white handkerchief, folded small, covered its eyes, but did not conceal the features, which waxy and pallid, death had composed into a smile. Though the child had been dead two days, it was unprovided with a coffin. The odour of the house was almost insupportable. Before the fire were three or four children; amongst them a boy named Martin B---, 11 years of age, who had been placed there by the parish, the allowance being 2 shs per week. This boy had no shirt; he was barefooted, in rags, his hair bristled up, and he was literally black with filth' (Ginswick, 1983, pp. 86, 87).

As pointed out by *The Cardiff and Merthyr Guardian* on 10 November 1849, it was not surprising that some of these children grew up to be the bullies of 'China' and the pest of every neighbourhood in the district. The savage treatment meted out in Merthyr Tydfil Police Court to children who broke the law, is reflected in the Quarter Sessions collection:

Robert Glendenning, aged 11 years, stole a cup worth 1d and 2 shillings in coppers, the property of Peter Price. On 16 July 1849, he was sentenced to one week's imprisonment for this offence.

Mary Evans, aged 13 years, stole one flannel apron worth 2 shillings, the property of James Thornton, and was sentenced on 29 June 1850 to 14 days' hard labour.

James Dacey, 11 years of age, stole 12 ozs of beef worth 5d, the property of William Harding, and was sentenced to a whipping on 5 January 1853.

Thomas Barry, $7\frac{1}{2}$ years old, in 1864 stole six rhubarb tarts worth 3d, the property of Mary Hopkins. On 28 May 1864, he was sentenced to 14 days' hard labour and four years in a reform school for this offence.
(Glamorgan Quarter Session list of Juvenile Convictions, vol. 1).

Such draconian punishments make tragic reading. While there are no means of knowing whether or not they were paupers, the fact remains that pauper children committing such offences would have incurred similar punishments in any case. It is worth tracing their treatment in some detail because it shows the ruthless, inflexible and hypocritical nature of some members of the Board of Guardians who professed support for the children but were reluctant to meet the cost of a separate school. Their condition was exposed by the rector, the Rev. J. C. Campbell, who may not have realised in March 1848 when he wrote to the Merthyr Tydfil Board about the problem, what a long fight lay ahead. He stated that he had long been aware of the deplorable condition of child paupers brought up in common lodging-houses amid scenes and with associations that were bound to have the most adverse effect on them. He appealed to the Guardians to take over the Old Brewery to house them and to send them to school when they were of age. He believed public subscriptions might be forthcoming for such a purpose. His final appeal expressed the spirit of the age: '*I am convinced that it is unnecessary for me to dwell longer on the advantages likely by God's blessing to arise from thus removing the children from an atmosphere both morally and physically unwholesome, and I am sure that even in a financial point of view, it would be of no small benefit to the Union that they should be well looked after and properly brought up, and fitted to fill with credit and usefulness the position, however humble, in which Providence has placed them*' (PRO MH12/16328 24 March 1848).

This letter occasioned a special meeting of the Board of Guardians on 24 April 1848 when it was decided to establish an asylum for pauper children not living with their parents, where they would be maintained at a rate of £8 per annum. On 6 May 1848, it was further decided to inspect the Old Brewery with a view to making it an asylum for vagrants as well as pauper children.

'*The following gentlemen were appointed as Committee to inspect and report upon the condition of the Brewery premises and their fitness for an asylum for orphan children and vagrant poor. Mr. Lewis Lewis, Mr. B. Martin, Mr. H. Kirkhouse, Mr. W. Richards, Mr. Jno Smith, Mr. David Davies, Mr. Wm Howell.*'   (Minutes MTBG, 6 May 1848).

That such an unfortunate combination of paupers would be placed together in a building with unsavoury associations, doomed the plan to failure. Inspector Andrew Doyle visited Merthyr Tydfil in May 1848 to look into the proposal (PRO MH12/16328, 9 May 1848). He inspected the lodging-houses where the pauper children were placed and concluded that the moral degradation was

Henry Austin Bruce.

appalling. He canvassed the rector, the stipendiary magistrate (H. A. Bruce), and some of the leading members of the Board of Guardians. Only when they convinced him that it was hopeless to attempt to provide a workhouse was he prepared to consider the Old Brewery as an asylum because he thought it might be a step in the right direction. Inspector Farnell attended the meeting of the Guardians at the end of May 1848 to discuss the arrangements for pauper children (PRO MH12/16328, 27 May 1848). His report to the Poor Law Board was revealing: he realised the importance of the subject but also understood the attitude of this Board of Guardians. His approach to them would be influenced by the spirit they showed, but he hoped to introduce a very different feeling from that which usually prevailed. '*Much may be done for Merthyr Tydfil then*'.

This persuasive approach did not yield the desired results. A committee set up to examine the Old Brewery did not carry out its work and did not report. Its members withdrew because they thought the premises unsuitable and the cost of conversion excessive. Inspectors Doyle and Farnell discouraged a scheme partly financed out of private subscriptions because it would produce divided authority and people would tire of paying. Instead, an attempt was made to use the problem of pauper children to force the Guardians to tackle the main question, a workhouse.

H. A. Bruce supported the Inspectors by arguing for a workhouse on the grounds of economy and humanity. Using the condition of pauper children as a powerful incentive, he dwelt at length on the utter degradation and squalor in which the 50-70 orphan children existed while in the care of the Board of

Duffryn House, Mountain Ash.

67

Guardians. He considered that since they were brought up with the most vicious and depraved habits and were trained to become thieves and prostitutes, they were being condemned to the greatest misery in the world. He appealed to the Guardians to balance the present and eternal welfare of these children against the small number of able-bodied paupers who would be driven into the workhouse when one was provided. After appeals to their hearts, heads and pockets, he managed to get a resolution passed by a majority of one '*That the interests of economy and humanity would be equally promoted by the erection of a workhouse*' (*CMG* 24 June 1848) (See Chapter 7).

Further delays ensued while discussions were held about the possibility of an industrial school where the children would not be influenced by the polluting effects of the workhouse (PRO MH12/16328, 14 April 1849). By this time, cholera and its dreaded consequences was absorbing the attention of the Board of Guardians, who diverted responsibility for the pauper children to the Poor Law Board by claiming that since they would not sanction an industrial school without a workhouse, the moral injury being done to the children was the fault of the Poor Law Board!

Later that same year, several ministers of religion and tradesmen petitioned the Guardians to erect an industrial school. '*The Union*', they said, '*through you, its legal and properly constituted authorities, is responsible to humanity and to God for the moral and industrial training of pauper children, and they beg most respectfully and earnestly to have erected and established without delay, an industrial school*' (*CMG* 10 Nov. 1849). But the special meeting of the Guardians called to discuss this question succeeded only in revealing the deep divisions and blind prejudices that existed among them. It was a well-attended meeting, the ironmasters and ratepayers having been given notice of the motion for discussion. The lip-service which had been paid to such a school vanished, to be overtaken by considerations of economy.

Two main factions emerged, one led by H. A. Bruce, and the other by John Evans of Dowlais, agent of Sir John Guest. Bruce proposed a resolution, '*That this Board do immediately appoint a committee to devise the best means of providing for the education of orphan children now dependent upon the Union, by the erection of an industrial school and the hiring and purchasing of land adjoining it*' (*CMG* 10 Nov. 1849). John Evans opposed it on the grounds that such schools might be suitable for agricultural areas but not for industrial ones. He considered that a school as proposed by H. A. Bruce, to accommodate 150 orphans and 121 illegitimate children, would be inadequate because there were 1,126 others living with their mothers who were widows. The best plan, he believed, would be to have a school attached to the proposed workhouse and he moved an amendment accordingly. Both the proposal and amendment were seconded. H. A. Bruce pointed out the disadvantages of putting children into a workhouse where it would be impossible to keep them apart from dissolute paupers. He emphasised that wherever this system had been tried, it had failed. His resolution was defeated by one vote, showing a distinct change of attitude by the Guardians who had previously professed support for an industrial school as a better and cheaper way of looking after orphan pauper children. Not to be beaten, Bruce and his supporters determined to re-open the matter in one month's time.

The Cardiff and Merthyr Guardian attacked this rejection of an industrial school with great ferocity on 8 June 1850. The question was asked why Merthyr Tydfil Union should repeat the mistake of including children in the workhouse when it had failed elsewhere and was condemned for '*deluging the country with sickly, useless, abject paupers*'. It was alleged that no respectable householder would take into his service and family a girl brought up in the workhouse; he knew only too well the low level of workhouse morality and the evil effect of workhouse habits to entrust his children or his property to a workhouse girl. It was alleged that on all sides these children would be repulsed with scorn or received with distrust. The only professions left to them would be theft and prostitution with which girls became acquainted in the workhouse. The 'abandoned women' who swarmed into workhouses made it impossible to stop such contamination. Evidence from Poor Law Board Inspectors was quoted to support these views: '*The accounts I received of the conduct of girls on leaving the workhouse were invariably favourable or unfavourable in the same measure as their separation from the able-bodied women was effectual or to the contrary ... but from the enquiries I have made, I am led to fear that a large proportion of those in urban unions fall into prostitution*'. Another Inspector stated, '*I believe an overwhelming mass of evidence exists as to the necessity of separating children from adult paupers. I have been expressly assured on authority which I cannot question, that they positively try to corrupt children in the workhouses*'.

This press campaign was timed to coincide with the re-opening of the question of the prevailing treatment of pauper children. It made an onslaught on the policy of the Board of Guardians by asking '*How in the name of common-sense, humanity and Christianity itself, the Guardians - reverend gentlemen, experienced magistrates, intelligent trademen and respectable farmers could reconcile it with their consciences to persist in a system fraught with the present and eternal ruin of these wretched victims of misfortune. It would be better to drown them in the deepest pool in the River Taff, or shovel them down the nearest abandoned coal pit, than educate them in this way for infamy and wretchedness. It would be far cheaper and more humane to do such a thing*'. These strong words were meant to shame and frighten the Guardians into making separate provision for the children, but they refused to be convinced, even though the cholera epidemic of the previous year had revealed such appalling conditions.

Orphan pauper children continued to be sent two or three at a time to the keepers of lodging-houses who contrived to make a profit from the miserable pittances paid for the children, and allowed them to run about the streets ragged and barefooted with children belonging to the most notorious characters. Often they were encouraged or compelled to beg. Their education was not even considered. If they died early, as, fortunately for them, often happened, so much the better for the parish. If they lived to an age when they could work, (i.e. 11 years of age), employment was sought for them at an ironworks when they were free to live as they pleased and spend their wages as they wished. Such a system bred poverty, crime and wickedness.

H. A. Bruce made one final attempt to rescue the children from these conditions and from the workhouse when, at a special meeting of the Board of Guardians called on 6 July 1850, he put forward the resolution that '*That the workhouse should be built without a school, and that when it was completed, an industrial school should be set up in Merthyr Tydfil Union'* (*CMG* 13 July 1850). It produced a bitter, tempestuous debate in which the two factions within the Board fought to a finish. Bruce tried to convince them of the need for these two separate institutions by pointing out the increased expenditure in the previous year and the increase in pauperism in the Union. This alone would justify setting up a school which would educate children out of pauperism. He quoted Inspectors' Reports from the Poor Law Board, all of which condemned the education of children within workhouses. His arguments, based on facts and logic, were meant to convince the Guardians of the desperate need for a separate school. He was supported by Robert Jones who made an impassioned plea in both English and Welsh on the grounds that since the orphans had no one else to protect them, the responsibility placed on the Guardians was enormous.

The factions began to reveal themselves when W. Rees of Llanfabon parish moved an amendment '*That a workhouse be built as in other parts of the country ... to provide school accommodation in the house'*. Asked to give his reasons, he touched

A Beggar Child. Illustration by George Cruikshank, 1847.

the heart of the matter when he said '*It appears that you are going to raise these children above what the ratepayers can manage, above what the ratepayers can maintain*'. Lewis Lewis, grocer and draper, Vice-Chairman of the Board of Guardians, admitted that the education of pauper children was important, but added that he was there to represent the ratepayers. They had already allocated money for a workhouse on top of which they were being asked to pay for a separate school. They had been accused of neglecting pauper children, but he had been present when pauper lists were revised and the children he saw were '*a credit to the world*'. Giving a side-kick to H. A. Bruce, he said that if pauper children were neglected, it was the fault of certain Guardians who should attend more often and not turn up to make speeches only when a newspaper reporter was present. He believed there were only four children in the 'cellars' and they had been born there, among them a child of the 'Queen of China' who belonged to Aberdare parish! He reiterated his belief that their pauper children were a credit to the world and pointed out that when the boys reached the age of 11, they were taken by the hand to the ironworks. He wanted to know what the ironmasters had to say about a separate school, because it was they who would have to put their hands into their pockets. He believed a workhouse should come first, as a separate school would only increase pauperism and attract children from all parts of Wales to Merthyr Tydfil.

Such fatuous arguments and unfounded fears were disposed of by H. A. Bruce who pointed out that Lewis Lewis had been the first person to tell him about the state of pauper children who went begging, barefoot, about the town. To prove the point, he referred to what had happened in the coldest part of the winter of 1849-50. Bruce's sister, Mrs. J. C. Campbell, wife of the rector of Merthyr Tydfil, had met a child on the steps of the schoolroom, who was half-naked, barefooted and black with cold. She took him into the schoolroom and revived him so that he could speak, and he proved to be the son of a woman to whom the Guardians had sent two pauper children. Mrs. Campbell gave the child warm clothing and sent him home. A few days later, she met the same child in the same condition, barefooted and half-naked. Bruce asked the question that if a mother could treat her own child in that way, how did the Guardians expect her to treat other people's children? He admitted that when this case was reported, the Relieving Officer removed the two pauper children from this woman, but to say that such a system no longer existed and had been altered, was untrue. The only reply Lewis could muster to this irrefutable argument was that it would always be so in a place like Merthyr Tydfil. Such cynicism and fatalism did not go unchallenged.

The Chairman of the Board of Guardians, D. W. James (of the radical James faction), pointed out that Lewis was mistaken when he said he was the representative of the ratepayers, he was simply one of them, because the ironmasters to whom he referred, represented themselves by their agents. Two of the ironmasters, Kirkhouse and Crawshay, had already stated they wanted a workhouse first and an industrial school afterwards. Ratepayers had petitioned for a school as part of the plan, and there was no petition against a school to provide industrial training for pauper children.

After such a heated debate, the vote was taken with a tied result: 12 for Bruce's motion, 12 for the amendment. The Chairman gave his casting vote for the proposition which was carried '*with loud cheers*'.

'*Moved by H. A. Bruce Esq. and Seconded by Mr. Robert Jones;*
That in the erection of the New Workhouse no accomodation shall be provided for the permanent pauper children belonging to the Union is being intended that they should be educated in a separate Industrial School.

Amendment moved by Mr. William Rees, Seconded by Mr. John Jones (Tophill)
That the Workhouse be built as in this and the adjoining counties that is to say to provide school accomodation for the children in the house

For the Motion	For the Amendment
D. W. James Esq.	Mr. Richard Davies
H. A. Bruce Esq.	Mr. John Williams
W. Thomas Esq.	Mr. Edward Thomas
Lewis Morgan Esq.	Mr. Griffith Davies
Mr. Robert Jones	Mr. David Jones
Mr. David Llewellyn	Mr. Phillip Phillips
Mr. John Smith	Mr. John Jones
Mr. David Davis	Mr. Lewis Jenkins
Mr. Morgan Morgan	Mr. Henry Kirkhouse
Mr. Rice Lewis	Mr. Lewis Lewis
Mr. George Roach	Mr. William Rees
The Revd. J. Griffith	Mr. Watkin Watkins

Neuter

Mr. William Thomas

Mr. D. W. James, Chairman, gave his casting vote in favour of the motion. Motion carried.'
(Minutes MTBG, 6 July 1850).

After a strenuous and prolonged fight, H. A. Bruce had proved his point, but as plans for the workhouse were prepared, it became clear that they included accommodation for pauper children who would be educated within the workhouse. Consideration of economy had triumphed. As the building neared completion, action was taken to remove pauper children '*from the cellars of Merthyr where they lodged with people of doubtful character*' (Minutes MTBG, 2 Oct. 1852). The Relieving Officers were ordered to make a return of all male children between the ages of four and ten, and female children between four and fourteen years who were likely to become members of the workhouse (Minutes MTBG, 30 April 1853). During the first six months, 155 children were placed in the workhouse. Not until 1876, was there a chance that an industrial school, separate and distinct from the workhouse, could be provided.

CHAPTER 7

The provision of a Workhouse

As outlined in the two previous chapters, the growing scandal of the orphan pauper children, and the serious consequences of typhus, smallpox and cholera epidemics, compelled the Board of Guardians to face the unpalatable truth that they would have to provide a workhouse. For seventeen years they had been able to pursue a policy of evasion; not until 1853 did the workhouse become a reality. The overall pattern emerges: 1836-1839, a period of superficial concern; 1839-1846, a period of inactivity; 1848-1853, a period of crisis and successful endeavour.

The first attempt to provide a workhouse was made by Assistant Commissioner Clive when he attended the meeting of the Board of Guardians on 12 November 1836. Having expounded the Poor Law Amendment Act of 1834, he went on to urge them to erect a workhouse (Minutes MTBG, 12 Nov. 1836). Initially, he gained the support of the Guardians who set up a committee to go into the matter, and by April 1837, a site had been selected at

View of Merthyr Tydfil, 1865. Published by Rock & Co., London.
The Workhouse is shown in the bottom right-hand corner.

Pontygwaith Farm, Merthyr Tydfil. The earliest entries relating to the building of a workhouse ran thus:

> '*Resolved that the following Gentlemen do form a Committee for the erection of a Workhouse.*
> *Rowland Fothergill Esq. M. Morgan Esq. W. Thomas Esq. Lewis Morgan Esq. Mr. Rowd. Hopkins Mr. T. Evans Mr. Martin Mr. Jenkins and Mr. Lewis Edwards, any three to be a quorum*'.
> (Minutes MTBG, 12 Nov. 1836).

> '*Ordered, that the Clerk write a letter to J. J. Guest Esqre., M.P. to inform him that part of Pontygwaith farm has been selected as a site for the Workhouse, by the Committee formed for that purpose, and to request him to ascertain from the Hon. Mr. Clive if he will dispose of the spot which has been selected.*'
> (Minutes MTBG, 8 Apr. 1837).

This land proved too expensive and other sites were then considered. On 10 June 1837, an architect presented plans to the Board of Guardians for a workhouse to accommodate 200 inmates at a total cost of £2,940 (Minutes MTBG, 10 June 1837). At a special meeting convened on 1 July 1837, it was decided to lease from the Hon. Mr. Clive, a piece of land near Pontygwaith bridge for one halfpenny per yard per annum, but negotiations came to an abrupt end.

Writing to the Poor Law Commissioners from Llandovery in Carmarthenshire on 28 August 1837, Assistant Commissioner Clive had to admit that the question of Merthyr Tydfil workhouse was abandoned and that he did not consider it wise to proceed until the strong feeling against it had abated (PRO MH12/16326, of that date). He reported that the recent elections in Glamorgan and Carmarthenshire had done incalculable harm to the New Poor Law. It was only with reluctance that the established Guardians carried on with their duties at all because of the intense unpopularity they faced, and for this reason they were slack in their administration of poor relief. Though disappointed with the slow progress of the new regime, he comforted himself with the thought that except for Merthyr Tydfil, all the other workhouses under his care were under construction.

Various abortive attempts were made to obtain a suitable site, and by January 1839, it seemed at last that Assistant Commissioner Senior had got them to move in the matter (PRO MH12/16326, 26 Jan. 1839). By dint of personal canvassing, he claimed to have '*screwed up*' the minds of the Board to go forward with a scheme immediately. He wanted the Central Commissioners to send an order of approval at once to the Guardians whom he compared with '*timid people in the dark, frightened by the least noise*'. Having brought them to the point of signing an order of consent for building a workhouse, he thought that speed was of the essence, as they would never sign another one. His efforts are reflected in these entries:

> '*Ordered that the Clerk apply to Mr. Morgan the ground landlord to ascertain if he will extend the lease of the land to 99 years from the present time and that he be directed to offer 2d. per yard after the expiration of the present term.*

Ordered that the Clerk be directed to write to Mr. Wilkinson the Architect to ascertain the difference in price for building a Workhouse to contain 100 paupers and another to contain 200, and to request Mr. Wilkinson to attend the meeting of the Board on Saturday the 14th July.'
(Minutes MTBG, 30 June 1838).

'Ordered that the Clerk write to Mr. Wilkinson, Architect, stating that the Board wishes him to obtain the Workhouse plans from the Poor Law Commissioners as early as possible and to forward them . . . at least one week before he shall arrive. Ordered that the Clerk provide the Parish Officers of Merthyr Tydfil with the forms relative to the Workhouse site which accompanied the Poor Law Commissioners' letter of the 14th inst.'
(Minutes MTBG, 16 Feb. 1839).

Bureaucracy intervened in the form of legal difficulties over the land, and the delay of two months proved fatal. On 20 February 1839, the Assistant Commissioner referred to the considerable excitement which existed in Merthyr Tydfil over the question of a workhouse and said that he had been told the Board of Guardians would be returned at the next election on their pledge of opposing the building of one (PRO MH12/16326, of that date).

The most burning resentment against the New Poor Law was felt in the industrial areas, where it was regarded as 'inhuman, monstrous, wicked and detestable'. Though complete destitution was not as general in manufacturing as in rural areas, most workers faced the possibility of requiring poor relief at some time in their lives, for they could save nothing from their weekly wages to meet unemployment, sickness or old age. To go to a parish officer for relief to tide them over was one thing, but to be forced into a workhouse was a very different matter. Despite assurances to the contrary, there was a widespread belief that all recipients of poor relief would be 'offered' the workhouse. The year 1836, when the Commissioners began their work, was the last of the good trade years, it was followed by a recession which made every worker fear the 'Bastille'. Moreover, the New Poor Law had come to the working class as the result of the Reform Act of 1832. In return for the common struggle they had made with the middle class, they had received the 'workhouse test' and the declaration that poverty was the fault of the poor. It was this betrayal that drove them into the demand for independent working-class action and prepared the ground for the Chartist movement.

Throughout 1838 there were demonstrations in support of the People's Charter with its six points: universal male suffrage; annual parliaments; the secret ballot; the removal of property qualifications for election to Parliament; salaried MPs. and equal electoral districts. In Merthyr Tydfil, plans were made for a rally at Penyrheolgerrig on Christmas Day, 1838 (*From Reform to the Charter*, Kevin Littlewood, 1990, pp. 25-27). The aims of the Charter were endorsed, and Hugh Williams was elected as the Chartist representative at the National Convention. The crowd then marched down into Merthyr Tydfil, past the captain of the militia, the magistrates and the special constables to the Market Square, where they dispersed peacefully. Chartism was to flare up again and die down in 1839, 1842 and 1848 as industrial depression and high food prices made their impact on the workers.

It is, therefore, not surprising that the Assistant Commissioners who visited Merthyr Tydfil Union failed to persuade the Board of Guardians to proceed with a workhouse. As late as 1847, fear of popular resistance was still the cause of delay and, as we have seen, the local press pointed out that no matter how necessary a workhouse might be, public opinion was too strongly opposed for the measure to be implemented (*CMG* 12 June 1847). Not even the widespread distress in the typhus epidemic of 1847, or the pitiful sufferings of orphan pauper children, could convince the Guardians that they should take such a step. The Poor Law Commissioners used every possible means of persuasion, including a warning of the dangers of the threatened crisis over the renewal of the Dowlais lease in 1848, to induce the Guardians to provide a workhouse, but the trade recession of 1848 and the fear of popular resistance still held them back. They were so evenly divided on the issue that no action could be taken until opposition within their ranks and public feeling outside had subsided. (See Ginswick, 1983, pp. 80-81).

By the end of the Forties, trade improved and Britain entered a period of prosperity. Wages rose and unemployment fell; as the workers enjoyed their share of this prosperity, so their support for Chartism drifted away. It was in these circumstances, and with the consequences of major epidemics of sickness in the Union to consider, that the Guardians squared up to the fateful decision about a workhouse.

The turning-point came at a meeting on 17 June 1848 (Minutes MTBG, of that date). Inspector Farnell attended on that occasion determined to bring the matter to a head. A full account of this momentous meeting also appeared in *The Cardiff and Merthyr Guardian* on 24 June 1848. The now famous motion was proposed by H. A. Bruce and seconded by D. W. James, '*That the interests of humanity and economy would be equally promoted by the erection of a work house*'. An amendment '*That the question be not entertained for the present*' was proposed and seconded by William Rees and William Richards who represented rural parishes within the Union. All the Guardians of the parishes of Merthyr Tydfil and Aberdare voted in favour of a workhouse, while those of the seven remaining parishes were against it. The following comment appeared in the local press: '*As, however, the parishes of Merthyr Tydfil and Aberdare contain a full three-quarters of the population of the whole Union, and as their Guardians may without offence be supposed to be better selected from a more intelligent and better-informed class than those of parishes which form the minority, and as, moreover, the majority was supported by the declared adhesion of the four largest ratepayers, the Dowlais, Cyfarthfa, Penydarren and Aberdare companies, this expression may be considered decisive*'. The resolution was carried by only one vote: 12 in favour, 11 against.

'*It was proposed by H. A. Bruce Esq. Seconded by D. W. James Esq.*

That the interests of humanity and economy would be equally promoted by the erection of a workhouse.

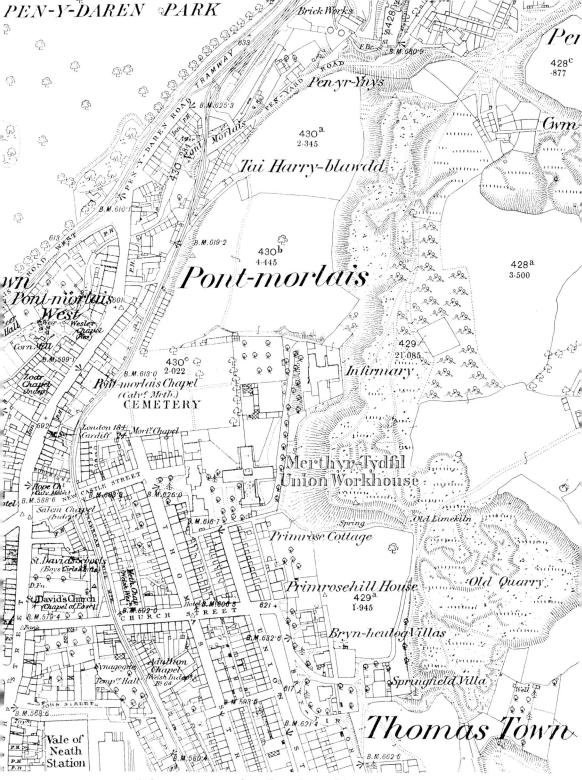

Ordnance Survey map of 1884 shows the site of the workhouse.

Moved by Mr. William Rees, Seconded by Mr. William Richards That the question be not entertained for the present: when there appeared

For the ammendment	For the Original motion
Mr. *William Rees*	Mr. *D. W. James*
" *John Williams*	" *Benjamin Martin*
" *Griffith Davies*	" *Henry Kirkhouse*
" *Richard Evans*	" *Lewis Lewis*
" *David Davis*	" *John Smith*
" *John Richards*	" *George Martin*
" *William Richards*	" *Richard Williams*
" *Morgan Rees*	" *Morgan Morgan*
" *William Miles*	*William Thomas Esqre.*
" *Lewis Thomas*	*H. A. Bruce Esqre.*
G. R. *Morgan Esqre.*	*E. A. Hutchins Esqre.*
	Mr. *William Howell*

being 11 for the ammendment and 12 for the original motion which was declared duly carried. And the Clerk was directed to forward a copy of the foregoing resolution to the Poor Law Commissioners with a request that the majority be permitted to carry out the same.

The following Gentlemen were appointed a Committee to ascertain whether any land could be purchased suitable for a workhouse:
Mr. Henry Kirkhouse, Mr. Benjamin Martin, Mr. John Smith, Mr William Rees, Mr. William Richards, H. A. Bruce Esqre., Mr. John Evans, William Thomas Esq.'
(Minutes MTBG, 17 June 1848).

Inspector Farnell had had to use all his powers of persuasion to produce this result. He had said that out of nine neighbouring Unions which had built 'poor-houses', expenditure which had been £44,000 in 1836 had been reduced by 1846 to £33,000, despite large increases in population. He singled out Abergavenny Union which showed very clearly the benefits to be expected and which he considered a fair comparision with Merthyr Tydfil. In 1841, it had a population of 50,674 whereas Merthyr Tydfil Union had 52,864. He explained that Abergavenny Union also included great industrial and manufacturing places such as Bedwellty, with extensive ironworks at Tredegar, Rhymney, Beaufort and Nantyglo. Whereas their average annual expenditure on poor relief was £6,817 in 1836, by 1841 it had fallen to £5,149, despite the increase in population. In contrast, the expenditure in Merthyr Tydfil Union in the three years ending 1840, averaged £6,214. In the three years ending 1847, it had increased to £8,897. For 1848, it was expected to amount to £12,110. The Inspector attributed this solely to the lack of a workhouse. He ignored the effects of the typhus and smallpox epidemics, the recession in the iron industry and the fear that the Dowlais Works would close. His main concern was to expound the virtues of a workhouse in combating pauperism. Yet again, he emphasised how expenditure had diminished by one quarter in all surrounding Unions despite an increase in population; only in Merthyr Tydfil Union had it increased by one-half. The logic of his argument was clear: workhouses produced economy. Even though the able-bodied were the main concern, he assured the Guardians that he had visited 18 workhouses recently and that he did not see one able-bodied man inside. *'The thing speaks for itself'*, he declared.

It was precisely this problem which worried many members of the Board of Guardians and produced animated discussion. In periods when trade was slack, many able-bodied workmen were only partly employed, and the Guardians were uneasy about forcing them into a workhouse in face of such difficulties. Inspector Farnell did his utmost to calm their fears and to placate them, by assuring them that though the letter of the law necessitated indoor relief only for such people, the Poor Law Board would allow them to use their discretion in such matters. This had a crucial effect on those present and decided the votes of the Chairman and Sir John Guest's representative, Hutchins, his nephew, who said that on no account would he have voted for a workhouse under the Poor Law as it first operated.

These practical considerations were reinforced by concern about the state of pauper children (see Chapter 6). As the local press summed it up: *'It is not surprising that after so many appeals to the head and to the heart, to sound reason and to kindly feeling, the majority of the Guardians should have pronounced in favour of the resolution. The great ratepayers, Guest, Thompson, Crawshay and Fothergill, all supported a workhouse. The Guardians of the country districts were the opposers but showed no bitterness on being beaten'* (CMG 24 June 1848).

A site for the workhouse was found at Cae-yr-odyn and after lengthy negotiations with the landowner (William Thomas of the Court) about the price to be paid, an agreement was signed on 29 September 1849 (Minutes MTBG, of that date). This was a period of great difficulty for the Board of Guardians owing to the severe cholera epidemic that afflicted the Union. Further controversy about a separate industrial school also delayed the workhouse. The Guardians were left to decide for themselves about this arrangement, as the Poor Law Board by this time was desperate to see a workhouse constructed as soon as possible. On 20 August 1849, the Guardians signed a consent form for a building to hold 500 people at a cost of £10,000 (Minutes MTBG, of that date).

Approaches were made to Guest, Crawshay, Thompson, Hill, Fothergill and Crawshay Bailey to ascertain whether they would lend money and at what interest. The only one to respond was Thompson who subsequently withdrew his offer and arranged for the Atlas Insurance Company to lend the sum at $4\frac{1}{4}\%$ (Minutes MTBG, 17 Aug. 1850). This was accepted, the union seal was affixed to the deed of loan, and £10,000 was paid over, of which £7,000 was put into a deposit account to earn 2% interest. Advertisements for plans were issued and members of the Workhouse Building Committee were empowered to visit other workhouses. On 3 October 1850, the Workhouse Committee and Inspector Hurst examined the plans and decided on one from Aickin and Capes of Islington.

'The Clerk read Mr. Gwilt's 2nd report (being on the 7 plans) when Resolved that the Clerk be directed to write to Messrs. Aickin & Capes, Islington, the Architects who sent in the plan for a Poor House under the signature of "Si

Ordnance Survey map of Pontystorehouse (China), 1884.

Fortuna Juvat" informing them that they are entitled to the premium of 20 guineas and that the Committee would be glad to see some one from their house at a meeting to be held on Saturday the 23rd inst. at 3 o'clock P.M. if they are desirous of superintending the erection of such a Workhouse as shall be determined upon.' (Minutes MTBG, 13 Nov. 1850).

The pace of construction of the workhouse was spasmodic. The foundation stone was laid without publicity. A small lime kiln was installed to burn lime for mortar, and the walls went up gradually (*CMG* 26 July 1851). The early progress by Messrs. Thomas and Norris, the builders, however, was not maintained, so that a year later, by which time all should have been completed, the Board of Guardians threatened to impose penalties (Minutes MTBG, 16 July 1852). The date when the workhouse building, for which Merthyr had waited for so long, was finally completed, was not however recorded in the minutes (See Appendix 13).

A modern view of the entrance to the former workhouse.

Officers for the workhouse were appointed on 5 March 1853, when Mr. and Mrs. Jones of Llanelly became Master and Matron at a salary of £50 and £30 per annum respectively. A schoolmistress was appointed on a temporary basis on 27 August 1853 at a salary of 20 guineas a year and double rations. The services of a doctor were obtained at a salary to be negotiated. Furniture, such as benches, tables and shelving, was ordered and advertisements for foodstuffs were issued. Two dozen hammers for breaking stones were ordered on 26 September 1853.

The exact date of opening is not known but would appear to have been during the last week in September 1853, when there was a noticeable fall in the amounts paid to Relieving Officers for outdoor relief and it was also decided that deserted families should have indoor relief only in future '*Moved by Rees H. Rhys, seconded by Mr. Lewis Lewis and Resolved as follows viz. That inasmuch as it is the opinion of this Board that granting Outdoor Relief to women and children who have been deserted by their husbands and fathers has a tendency to increase the number of such cases, Resolved That no relief will henceforward be granted to Paupers of this class except by admission to the Workhouse*' (Minutes MTBG, 10 Sep. 1853). From 17 September 1853, meetings of the Board of Guardians were held in the workhouse which Inspector Hirst visited on 24 September 1853.

By 1 October, the paupers were complaining they did not have enough to eat and it was found necessary to install 'refractory cells'. The formal handing over of the workhouse took place on 10 December 1853. Although it could hardly have been described as excessive in size for such a large union, yet, such was the unpopularity of this institution that it was not one-third full by December 1853. Christmas dinner was provided for the inmates: '*Ordered that all the Inmates of the Workhouse have Roast Beef and Plum Pudding for dinner on Christmas day next, and that the Men and Women have 1 Pint of Beer each and the Boys $\frac{1}{2}$ Pint each*' (Minutes MTBG, 17 Dec. 1853).

CHAPTER 8

Life in the Workhouse

As previously stated, the 'workhouse test' was the practical means of enforcing the principle of 'less eligibility', consequently life in the workhouse was meant to be disagreeable and unattractive to supplicants for poor relief. The Poor Law Commissioners favoured 'one strong efficient building' as much like a prison as possible. As one of the Assistant Commissioners, Sir Francis Head, stated 'The very sight of a well-built, efficient establishment would give confidence to the Board of Guardians; the sight and weekly assemblage of all servants of their Union would make them proud of their office . . . while the pauper would feel it was utterly impossible to contend against it' (Longmate, 1974, p. 87).

The most common design for a workhouse was one in which the surrounding boundary walls formed a square within which was a two-storey building with an extra block in front for the waiting-hall, the porter's lodge and the Board Room. Most workhouses seemed to be designed to cut off inmates from the outside world by having small windows at least six feet above ground and a high wall around them.

> '*Ordered that Iron bars be placed up and down in the ablebodied men's rooms downstairs and crossways in the children's rooms, by Mr. Sims at the prices of the bars on the store rooms.*
> *Ordered that the Clerk write to Superintendent Wrenn, requesting him to send a Policeman to protect the Workhouse on Sunday*' (Minutes MTBG, 20 Aug. 1853.)

> '*Resolved that Iron Spikes should be put on the walls where required to prevent paupers going over.*'

> '*Resolved that the Master should lock the Doors on Sunday so that strangers be prevented from rambling over the House without leave.*'
> (Minutes MTBG, 7 March 1856).

Unfortunately, the original plan for Merthyr Tydfil workhouse seems not to have survived completely but the building conformed roughly to the above description. A special Committee scrutinised various plans which were submitted and the successful one had to be amended to provide an entrance lodge, offices and more accommodation for children (Minutes MTBG, 15 Feb. 1851).

It was intended that there should be careful segregation into various classes of paupers and that they should be kept absolutely separate. The Commissioners identified the following categories:

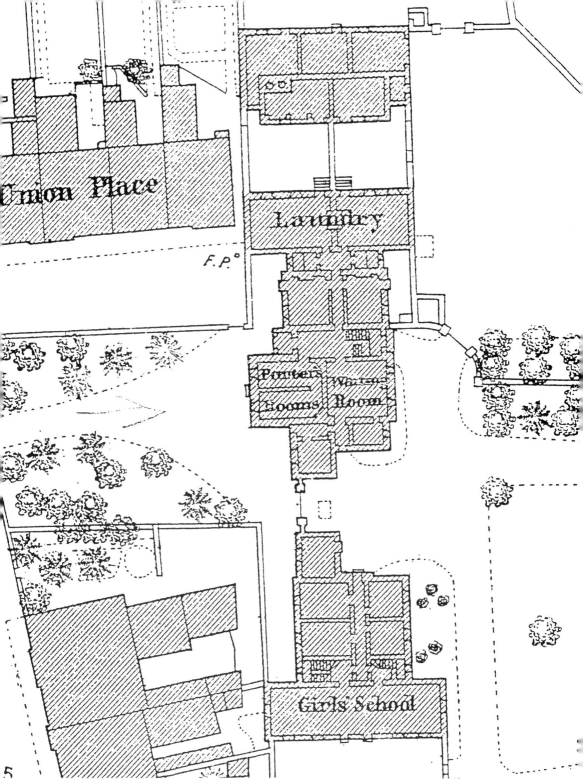

Ordnance Survey plan showing ancilliary offices and rooms.

Union Workhouse

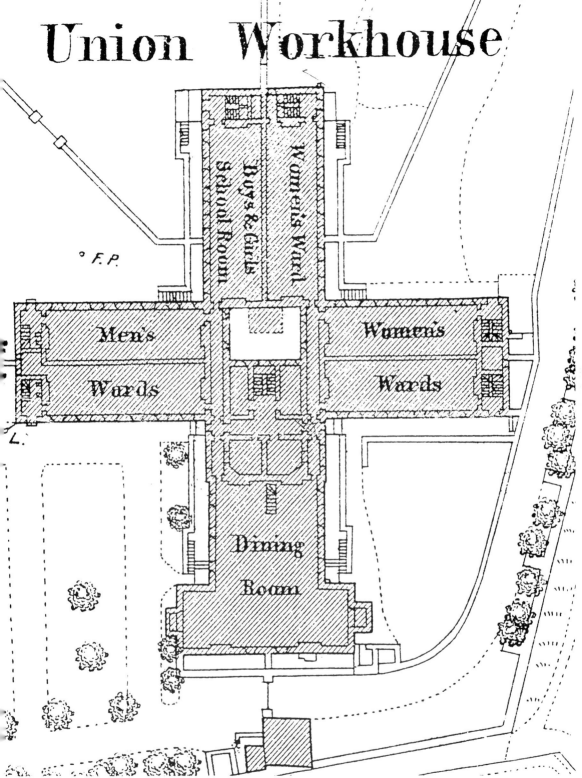

Men's Wards

Boys & Girls School Room

Women's Ward

Women's Wards

Dining Room

° F.P.

Ordnance Survey plan showing central block of workhouse.

A women's ward, with the crippled, aged and mental defective together. Drawing by
John Leech from the novel *Jessie Phillips, A Tale of the Present Day*, by Mrs. Trollope, 1844.

TABLE 11

Men infirm through age or any other cause
Able-bodied males over 15 years
Boys aged 7 - 15
Women infirm through age or any other cause
Able-bodied females over 15 years
Girls aged 7 - 15
Children under 7

The one concession made was that infants could remain with their mothers
until they were old enough to go to school at 3 or 4 years of age.

Furniture in the workhouse was basic and the least expensive possible, having
regard to durability. Cheap wooden or iron-framed beds, with flock or straw-
filled mattresses, pillows and two or three blankets, were the standard provision. Beds were tightly packed together so that only by climbing over the end,
could the occupant get in or out. The dining room had rough wooden tables

A meeting of a Board of Guardians. An applicant, weak from hunger, has fainted while presenting her case. Drawing by John Leech in *Jessie Phillips, A Tale of the Present Day*, 1844.

and backless benches. Notices of Regulations were the only items on the walls, diet tables and rules relating to workhouse life. No books or newspapers were provided and there were no games or toys for children. It is no wonder that mischief and boredom took over.

The daily time-table was laid down:

TABLE 12

Rising bell: March – September: 5.00 a.m.
Rising bell: October – February: 7.00 a.m.
Breakfast, preceded by prayers: 6.00 – 7.00 a.m. (Winter: 7.00 – 8.00 a.m.)
Work: 7.00 a.m. – 12.00 noon
Dinner: 12.00 – 1.00 p.m.
Work: 1.00 p.m. – 6.00 p.m.
Supper: 6.00– 7.00 p.m.
Prayers and to bed by 8.00 p.m. at the latest.

(*The Workhouse*, N. Longmate, 1974, p. 92).

A modern view of the workhouse chapel, which was also used as a dining room.

This dreary, boring routine coupled with hard, monotonous work, was meant to be thoroughly disagreeable. Oakum-picking in the male workrooms, and stone-breaking in the yards, were the forms of task work for the able-bodied males which Merthyr Tydfil workhouse provided. (Oakum consisted of old ropes, some tarred and knotted, which were cut into lengths to be unravelled, inch by inch, using fingers only, which became rough and raw). Before introducing oakum-picking, the Board of Guardians sent the Clerk and Workhouse Master to Swansea Gaol and Workhouse to see what methods they had adopted. A ton of 'junk' was then bought, and able-bodied men were set to work on it (Minutes MTBG, 29 March 1856). Women and girls were given housework of various forms, much of it unskilled, hard and tedious.

On admission, paupers were stripped of their own clothes, given a bath and a short hair-cut, and made to wear workhouse clothes which were usually crudely-made in a 'tailoring-shop' within the workhouse. Shoes were issued

New entrants were stripped and bathed. Drawn by Gustave Doré, *circa* 1870.

(which later came from a work-shop within the Industrial School at Aberdare). As under-clothing, the women had a shift (petticoat), drawers and long stockings. Men had thick vests, woollen drawers and socks. In cold weather, men were given a rough jacket. Children's clothes were usually coarse and unshapely, and their shoes were badly fitting. Baths were taken once a week. Men were not allowed razors so that they were shaved once a week, and a standard hair-cut was provided for each of the sexes.

The workhouse diet was plain and basic:

TABLE 13
DIETARY FOR THE ABLE-BODIED

		BREAKFAST		DINNER				SUPPER		
		Bread	Gruel	Cooked Meat	Rice	Potatoes	Cheese	Bread	Soup or Broth	Cheese
		Ozs.	Pints	Ozs.	Pints	Lbs.	Ozs.	Ozs.	Pts.	Ozs.
Sun.	Men	7	1½		1½			7		2
	Women	6	1½		1½			6		2
Mon.	Men	7	1½	4		I		7	1½	
	Women	6	1½	3½		I		6	1½	
Tues.	Men	7	1½		1½	I	2	7	1½	
	Women	6	1½		1½	I	2	6	1½	
Weds.	Men	7	1½	4		I		7	1½	
	Women	6	1½	3½		I		6	1½	
Thurs.	Men	7	1½		1½	I	2	7		2
	Women	6	1½		1½	I	2	6		2
Fri.	Men	7	1½	4		I		7	1½	
	Women	6	1½	3½		I		6	1½	
Sat.	Men	7	1½		1½	I	2	7	1½	
	Women	6	1½		1½	I	2	6	1½	

Old people of 60 and upwards could be allowed 1 oz of tea, 7 ozs of sugar, and 5 ozs of butter per week, in lieu of porridge, and also cheese for breakfast, if it was deemed expedient to allow this change (Minutes MTBG, 3 Sept. 1853).

As diets went, this one was less harsh than many. At all meals, women were given less bread than men, and the only drink for both sexes was water. Luxuries such as tea, butter and sugar were provided only for aged paupers. It is interesting to note that the diet for able-bodied men was far less than the prison ration of 292 ounces of solid food per week. The quality of workhouse food was poor and the gruel which was given for breakfast was particularly disliked, consisting as it did of thin oatmeal porridge, unflavoured with sugar or milk. Workhouse bread was invariably coarse and unpalatable.

Christmas in the workhouse. Painting by Hubert von Herkomer.

The separation of husbands from wives, and mothers from children, was supposed to be rigidly enforced. A husband who crossed the dining hall to speak to his wife could be punished both for breaking the rule of silence at meals and for fraternising with the opposite sex. Since they were not allowed outside the workhouse, unless they left permanently, they could not go to church or chapel. Arrangements were therefore made for Church of England clergymen and nonconformist ministers to conduct services within the workhouse. It was the sheer unrelenting boredom of workhouse life which was the worst punishment for most inmates, especially for children. (See Appendix 6).

In its early years, Merthyr Tydfil Workhouse had an uneasy existence because of the poor calibre of its officers. The first master and matron caused so many problems that it was necessary to appoint a committee of enquiry (Minutes MTBG, 7 July 1855). The facts that emerged were startling. The master was said to be far too lax in his duties, the matron was bad-tempered and neglectful, and the nurse was disagreeable and difficult. Workhouse discipline was too slack: there was insufficient separation of the classes of paupers, the master did not supervise the eating of meals in the dining hall and he neglected to call a register of paupers each morning and to inspect them. On several occasions, the women had frequented the men's bedrooms late at night and gross improprieties had taken place in the old men's day room. Though the matron had been present when some of these incidents occurred, she had not reported them. The master was frequently absent overnight without permission, and was out as late as 10 or 11 p.m., whereas doors were supposed to be locked at 9 p.m. (See Appendix 7). As a result of this report, the nurse was dismissed, and the master and matron resigned of their own accord. However, further difficulties ensued, the next master and matron holding office for barely a month before being asked to resign on account of drunkenness (Minutes MTBG, 20 Dec. 1855).

Even after the opening of the workhouse in 1853, the bulk of the poor relief administered in Merthyr Tydfil Union remained outdoor relief. Between 1853 and 1894, the number of outdoor paupers was generally many times greater than those in the workhouse but little concern was shown about their condition. From September 1853, the main attention centred on the workhouse and its functioning. (See Appendix 8).

PAUPER CHILDREN

As previously stated, pauper children were one of the largest classes of paupers. Referring to the scale of the problem, H. A. Bruce pointed out that in 1852, out of 2,888 people receiving relief in the Union, 1,514 were children under the age of sixteen: 299 lived with their parents, 809 were the children of widows, 88 were illegitimate, 19 had parents in gaol, 118 were orphans, and the rest could be accounted for. One hundred at least were engaged in petty thieving, and few were sent to school, as the Guardians had not assumed that responsibility (CMG 5 March 1853).

Though the Poor Law Board admitted that the general workhouse was no place for pauper children, they were sent there in September 1853. On admission, they were given the following allowances of food:

TABLE 14

Dietary Table A - Children 2 to 5

| | BREAK-FAST | | DINNER | | | | | SUPPER | | | |
| | Bread | Gruel | Meat | Potatoes | Rice Pudding | Bread | Cheese | Bread | Broth | Soup | Cheese |
	Ozs.	Pts.	Ozs.	Lbs.	Pts.	Ozs.	Ozs.	Ozs.	Pts.	Pts.	Ozs.
Sun.	4	½			I			4			I
Mon.	4	½	2	½				4	½		
Tues.	4	½			I			4		I	
Weds.	4	½	2	½				4	½		
Thurs.	4	½			I			4	½		
Fri.	4	½	2	½				4	½		
Sat.	4	½				4	I	4	½		

Dietary Table B - Children 5 to 9

| | BREAK-FAST | | DINNER | | | | | SUPPER | | | |
| | Bread | Gruel | Meat | Potatoes | Rice Pudding | Bread | Cheese | Bread | Broth | Soup | Cheese |
	Ozs.	Pts.	Ozs.	Lbs.	Pts.	Ozs.	Ozs.	Ozs.	Pts.	Pts.	Ozs.
Sun.	5	I			I			5			1 ½
Mon.	5	I	2 ½	½				5	I		
Tues.	5	I			I			5		I	
Weds.	5	I	2 ½	½				5	I		
Thurs.	5	I			I			5	I		
Fri.	5	I	2 ½	½				5	I		
Sat.	5	I				5	1 ½	5	I		

| Soup | Quantity per gallon | |
Ingredients	Ozs.	Pts.
Beef. .	12	8
Peas . .	13	8
Onions .	4	8

Broth
Made from what the meat was boiled in with an addition of bones cut out from the meat, and thickened with oatmeal and onions

Gruel		
	Ozs.	Pts.
Oatmeal...	18	8

(PRO MH12/16330, 25 Oct. 1856).

Rice Pudding sweetened with treacle		
	Ozs.	Pts.
Rice ...	21	8

The Guardians were urged by the Poor Law Board to increase the diet of children aged 5-9, but the Guardians refused to alter it for those aged 2-5 because of the difficulty of getting good milk in the winter-time.

One of the most important aspects of the care of children was their education in the workhouse school. The problems which arose confirmed the worst fears of H. A. Bruce; in general, such education was of the poorest quality. It was left to Boards of Guardians to start it as early or as late as they chose in the child's career. It was supposed to consist of at least three hours a day in reading, writing and Christian religion, as well as *such other instructions calculated to train them to habits of usefulness, industry and virtue*'. Arithmetic was not added to the list until 1842. Under the Poor Law Commissioners, the appointment of a school-master or school-mistress was optional, and no qualifications were asked for. Later, grants were paid for the salaries of qualified teachers in workhouse schools, and for this reason, from 1848 inspectors examined the schools and the teachers before the grant was paid.

A modern view of the boys' and girls' schoolrooms on the ground floor, women's wards on the first floor and children's dormitories and the lying-in ward on the second floor.

Oliver asks for more. Cruikshank's illustration in *Oliver Twist*, 1838.

From the outset, Merthyr Tydfil Board of Guardians experienced considerable difficulty in staffing the school. The first school-mistress, who was appointed at a salary of 20 guineas per annum and double rations, was unsatisfactory. Inspector Symons examined the workhouse school on 27 December 1853 and was so critical that he was not prepared to recommend it for a grant (PRO MH12/16329, 27 Dec. 1853). The 20 children in the school were described as '*backward, neglected and dirty*'. The school-mistress considered Inspector Symons had been unfair to her because at the time of his visit books had been available for only two or three weeks. Nevertheless, she was dismissed. When he next visited the school on 12 August 1854, he found that out of 27 boys and 17 girls, only 13 could read. The rest of the children were uninstructed and received far less than the three hours daily tuition required. Once again the grant was refused.

A sub-committee which was then set up to investigate the problem confirmed all the worst fears of the critics of the school. In the first place, neither of the two school-mistresses possessed any qualifications. Of 60 children in the workhouse, only 36 went to school, of whom only 18 were able to read and eight to spell. No attempt was made to teach them anything but reading. The Guardians tried to repudiate the charge of total neglect, preferred against them by Inspector Symons, by saying that some of the children were very young and that others had been there for only a short time, having been neglected before admission. However, they had to admit that girls had been made to do domestic work in the workhouse instead of being sent to school. It was decided to ensure that in future all children should attend school from 9.00 a.m. to 12.00 noon, and that it would remain open in the afternoon (PRO MH12/16329, 19 Aug. 1854).

A modern view of St. Tydfil's Hospital showing the separate workhouse school for girls with its adjoining yard.

The number of pupils continued to increase, and by March 1855 reached 202, so that it became necessary to provide a new schoolroom in the workhouse. Inspector Symons offered to find a suitable schoolmaster, whom the Guardians accepted, but even he proved unsatisfactory, and after an adverse report on his work by the Inspector, he resigned. His successor, appointed in November 1855, was reprimanded for not keeping himself or the children clean. He left, to be followed by a third, appointed on 21 September 1856, and dismissed on 3 October 1857, for making serious charges against the workhouse master. There was some improvement with the passage of time. Inspector Symons visited the school in July 1858 and considered that the school-master qualified for a third-class certificate which enabled the Guardians to obtain £32 10s.0d. for his services. The school-mistress was considered worthy of a second-class certificate which brought in a grant of £20 0s.0d. per annum. Symons was satisfied with the boys' section of the school (24 boys), but complained of the overcrowding in the girls' areas (63 girls) (PRO MH12/16331, 13 July 1858). As the Guardians were unwilling to pay for extra assistance, they brought an inmate of the workhouse, Bridgit Beazley, aged 14, to help the school-mistress. She had been a domestic help for six years and had spent some time in the workhouse school; she was given officers' rations and pocket money for assisting in the school.

The first book order of any importance was sent off to the Poor Law Board for approval on 26 July 1856:

TABLE 15

2 dozen	"No. 1 History of England" (1847) by Rev. A. Wilson Published by The S.P.C.K. at 1/– each	24/–
6 dozen	"The First Book", The Irish Board at ½d. each	3/–
1 dozen	"The Third Book", The Irish Board at 6d. each	6/–
1 dozen	"The Fourth Book", The Irish Board at 7d. each	7/–
1 dozen	"An Attempt to simplify English Grammar" by Sullivan at 6d. each	6/–
1 copy	"Geography Generalised" at 1/3d.	1/3
1 copy	"The Spelling Book Superseded" at 8d.	8
1 map of England by Messrs Chambers		8/–
		55/11d.

(PRO MH12/16330, 26 July 1856).

These English and Irish resources were to be the means of educating the 35 boys and 42 girls in the workhouse school at that time. The industrial training considered necessary to enable pauper children to become useful members of society took the form of washing and ironing for the girls and tailoring for the boys. On the advice of Inspector Brown, the Guardians appointed an officer to teach tailoring at a salary of £39 a year (PRO MH12/16333, 3 Oct. 1868).

The health of the children was never very good. Thus it was reported by the House Surgeon on 10 October 1863, that 72 girls were suffering from scabies. This he attributed to lack of cleanliness and overcrowding in the dormitories, where they slept three in a bed. It was decided to ensure that the dormitories were better ventilated, to provide adequate washing facilities nearby, and to improve the girls' diet. An outbreak of 'itch' occurred in July 1872, those infected being sent to the workhouse infirmary to be isolated from the rest. To improve their general health, the girls were to be taken for a daily walk, though this was later reduced to three times a week (Minutes MTBG, 20 July 1872).

Some of the girls received industrial training at Ely Industrial school, Cardiff, after that Union offered to take 20 pauper children in 1862 for a fee. To remove them from the polluting atmosphere of the workhouse, it was decided to try this experiment, which worked well.

> '*Read letter of Clerk of Cardiff Union stating that the probable share of Establishment Charges would be from 1/3 to 1/6d per head per week for children in the Industrial School.*
>
> *Resolved That it is expedient to send 20 girls to the Cardiff Industrial School and that the Clerk communicate to that Union accordingly, and that the Visiting Committee be requested to select the girls that are to go.*'
> (Minutes MTBG, 9 Jan. 1864).

From December 1865 to November 1869, all girls over the age of seven were sent from Merthyr Tydfil Workhouse to Ely Industrial school. An inspector commented that in every case where a child had not been left too long in the workhouse before being moved to Ely school, the results were excellent. The arrangement broke down when, in November 1869, the Cardiff Board of Guardians wanted to send a girl of 16 back to Merthyr Tydfil from Cardiff workhouse. As she had been sent to Ely school at the age of two, the Merthyr Tydfil Guardians considered that she had gained the status of irremovability and refused to accept her. The implications of this decision resulted in the Cardiff Guardians refusing to take any more Merthyr Tydfil children, and they asked that those already in the school should be removed (Minutes MTBG, 27 Nov. 1869). It was tragic that such a successful scheme should have been wrecked by a narrow, bureaucratic attitude.

While the girls had been sent to Ely, the boys below the age of seven had been put into the girls' section of the workhouse school. Those over seven years were sent to the National School in Merthyr Tydfil. Once they reached the age of 10 or 12, they were sent to work in local industries, though one of the inspectors considered that they should not be allowed to start work until they actually reached the age of 12 (PRO MH12/16333, 13 May 1865). When they started work, they ceased to be the responsibility of the Board of Guardians and had to fend for themselves.

It is not surprising that, in view of the unsatisfactory condition of the children in the workhouse and the overcrowding which occurred after 1869, the Guardians should have looked for an alternative solution. The course they took was boarding out, the very practice which had given rise to such problems before the workhouse was opened. '*Resolved - That this Board is of opinion that our Orphan and deserted children should be boarded out with Outdoor relief, so far as respectable and trust worthy householders can be found from time to time to receive them*' (Minutes MTBG, 19 July 1869). Popular at this time, it was 'idealised' as the answer to so many problems, but the fact remained that it was also the cheapest method of providing relief. In July 1870, a committee from the Board of Guardians considered the matter (Minutes MTBG, 2 July 1870). At this time there were 125 orphans, 44 illegitimate children and 101 legitimate children in the workhouse, making a total of 270. The Committee believed that they would be far better off outside, '*thus severing the connection between them and the idle and worthless persons who become inmates of these establishments*'. It was considered that the change would be for '*the good of the children, for the good of the Christian society of this land, as well as for the pecuniary advantages of the ratepayers of the district*'. The alternative of providing an industrial school was considered, but on balance, the boarding out system was favoured subject to certain safeguards. The Committee also thought that '*next to domicile with a parent . . . boarding out secured the greatest advantages for a child . . . All the constant industry and thrift which a laborious family is bound to pursue are brought constantly before the child, and there is besides, the watchful eye of the foster parent and the daily lessons in the battle of life, teaching prudence and propriety of conduct*'. In this way they sought to justify a scheme which was cheap, but, at the very least, unpredictable.

An attempt on 10 September 1870 to put forward a proposal for the construction of an industrial school was defeated and the boarding-out system was adopted. The terms on which this was to be done were outlined in the minutes of the Board of Guardians on 24 September 1870. People boarding children should '*train them in habits of industry, truth and honesty, and promise that they should attend some fit school, and, on Sunday, undertake some form of worship*'. Foster parents should receive not more than 3/- a week for each child below 10 years of age. School fees for all children should be paid by the Guardians. Each child should be provided with an outfit of clothes, and an allowance of 6/6d. quarterly should be paid for their clothes. Medical Officers would provide the necessary medical treatment. At first only orphans would be boarded out, and not more than two children placed in the same household, but despite all these elaborate plans, the scheme was not a success. Doubtless, there was difficulty in finding suitable homes, added to which there was a wariness about taking in children who were 'polluted' by the workhouse, and there was also the formidable problem of supervision. The result was that large numbers of children remained in the workhouse though some were given a chance to emigrate.

A scheme for emigration was started in 1872 with the selection of six girls sent to Canada (Minutes MTBG, 20 July 1872). Aged between 8 and 13 years, they were interrogated before a magistrate. The Guardians agreed to spend not more than £10 on each of the children, which was much less than the cost of keeping them in the workhouse. Six more were sent out on 22 March 1873, and five on 6 June 1874, after which time the practice fell out of favour.

'*We the Emigration Committee beg to report as follows*
1. *We have met and examined all the children of suitable age.*
2. *We annex a list of 6 children fit to emigrate with particulars relating to each.*
3. *We have requested the Surgeon to make a report upon each child which will also be annexed to this report.*
4. *The Statute limits the expence to £10 per child for emigration. The passage fee will be £8, we putting the children on board. We annex a list of clothing etc. which will have to be provided for each child.*'
(Minutes MTBG, 5 Sep. 1872).

Conditions in the workhouse at this time were far from satisfactory. Emphasising the gross inadequacy of the whole building for a Union of the size

Scene in a workhouse women's yard, *circa* 1840.

of Merthyr Tydfil, Inspector Doyle concentrated his attention on the children (PRO MH12/16335, 29 Oct. 1872). There were four dormitories capable of holding 80 children, though there were as many as 94 girls there at any one time. They slept two in a bed, and young girls were even placed among adult paupers. The state of the boys was worse, as it was completely impossible to separate them from the adults. In hospital, young children were forced to associate with men and women of doubtful character, and the Inspector considered that it would be difficult to exaggerate the evil effects of such associations.

The school-rooms were always overcrowded, with one teacher being responsible for 85 children—an impossible task (PRO MH12/16335, 23 Sep. 1871). Facilities for industrial training were unsatisfactory. One of the tramp wards had been converted into a 'wash-house', but to get there, the girls had to pass the Receiving Ward which was usually occupied by cases of infectious diseases. To get to their school-room, the girls had to pass through the men's yard or go through the women's department, so that they had close contact with adult paupers. The children were frequently attacked by 'itch', known to be prevalent for at least five months of the year. Commenting on the total inadequacy of these these arrangements, Dr. Clutterbuck, Inspector of Workhouse Schools, marvelled that the teachers were able to maintain any discipline at all because of 'the extremely prejudicial view of the adults upon the children' (PRO MH12/16337, 2 Feb. 1876).

All that H. A. Bruce had prophesied in 1849 had happened, but it had taken twenty-seven years to prove it. Concern about economy was always uppermost in the minds of the Guardians who believed that an industrial school would be 'a large palatial structure which however pleasing it may be to the eye, was not suited for the abode of children who in after life are to earn their living by their own labour' (Minutes MTBG, 2 July 1870).

Owing to public prejudice, the failure of a hospital in Aberdare in 1875 provided the opportunity to improve the lot of pauper children. From one failure came success of a different kind. Within six months of the hospital opening, Inspector Bircham had seized on the idea that because of its structural defects and unsuitability as a hospital it might be possible to convert it into an industrial school (PRO MH12/16337, 28 Aug. 1875). He canvassed some of the most influential members of the Board of Guardians, including Rees H. Rhys, who proposed that 'In the opinion of this Board, it is desirable that the Aberdare Hospital should cease to be used as a hospital and should be converted into an Industrial School for Pauper Children of the Union'. This was agreed unanimously on 13 May 1876.

The treatment they received is worth examining in detail because of the dramatic change in their condition by the end of the period under review. Compared with the pathetic state in which they existed before a workhouse and a separate school were provided, great progress was made once they were given separate accommodation. Generous staffing provision was made in the Industrial School: a Superintendent and Head School-master at a salary of £66 per annum; a Matron at £30; an Assistant School-master at £45; an Assistant

School-mistress at £25; a part-time Drill and Bandmaster at £10, an industrial trainer for girls, a Cook and a Dairymaid at £15; a Laundress at £17 and the services of a Medical Officer were also obtained as required. Dr. Clutterbuck, Inspector of Workhouse Schools, laid down principles for the Board of Guardians to follow at the school (PRO MH12/16337, 18 Oct. 1876). He pointed out that of the children then in the workhouse, only 19 were orphans, 12 were deserted, and the rest, numbering 92, were casuals. The problem of allowing parents to visit their children undermined the influence of the school and had to be watched carefully. Dr. Clutterbuck's poor opinion of the parents and children was clearly shown when he wrote, '*In an industrial district like Merthyr Tydfil, it is particularly necessary to train the children of the working class in habits of self-denial and providence and, wherever possible, to check the development of a communistic spirit*'. Was he referring to the industrial strife that characterised Merthyr Tydfil and Aberdare at that time or was he merely reflecting the prevailing official attitude towards poverty?

Rees H. Rhys, known as 'Blind Rhys'.

The Inspector also had strong views about teachers in the school. '*None but teachers thoroughly competent to train the children morally, as well as intellectually, should be entrusted with so grave a responsibility. As is the teacher, such is the pupil, and this is especially true of the easily-moulded children of poverty*'. Another Inspector, Bircham, hastened to reassure the Local Government Board, which had taken charge of Poor Law and Public Health in 1871, that there was no need for anxiety about parents influencing the children on account of the distance between Merthyr Tydfil and Aberdare (PRO MH12/16337, 5 Nov. 1876).

By April 1877, the school was ready for occupation with accommodation for 60 girls and 60 boys. Initially, there were only 48 girls and 9 boys in residence, but the numbers grew later. Emphasising the practical training component, the Superintendent submitted to the Industrial School Committee an outline of the instruction offered by the school (Hosp. & Trng. Sch. Comm. Min. Bk. 20 April 1877). Children were admitted from the age of five, but taking nine as the age when they were fit to work, he drew up what he considered would be suitable training. For the girls, it would be domestic work: six to clean the dormitories, four to work in the kitchen, two to clean the day room and closet, six to work in the laundry and four to wait at table and undertake other household tasks. Every afternoon, except Wednesday and Saturday, they should be taught needlework by the Matron. The boys were given a combination of indoor domestic duties and gardening: two to look after the boys' day room and closet and to clean the knives and forks, two to answer the bell, enter the names of visitors, go to the post and run errands; eighteen should be taught gardening by the farm bailiff. In wet weather, or during winter months, they should have extra lessons or be taught to make mats. All the children were to be divided into two classes which would take work and school on alternate days of the week. At least 18 hours a week would be given to reading, writing, arithmetic, religious instruction and '*such other instruction that shall produce in them habits of industry and virtue and promote their future usefulness and welfare*'.

Provision was made for their spiritual needs by allowing the vicar of Aberdare to hold services every Sunday morning at any time before 12.00 noon at the school. Nonconformist ministers were invited to attend every Sunday afternoon, and the Roman Catholic priest was allowed to visit on Wednesday afternoon each week from 2.00 - 3.30 p.m. Children were also given permission to attend the Roman Catholic church, subject to their being escorted to and fro. Those not catered for by these means were given half-an-hour of scripture stories each day by the Superintendent.

At first, the Guardians were mainly concerned with industrial training. They appointed a farm labourer to teach gardening and agricultural work (Hosp. & Trng. Sch. Comm. Min. Bk. 6 July 1877). A bailiff's cottage, cowshed and piggeries were acquired and three-quarters of an acre of land was sown with carrots and parsnips, three and a quarter acres with oats and vetches, one acre with potatoes, three acres with barley. Nine cows, two horses, and several pigs were bought for the farm. It was intended to supply milk to the workhouse

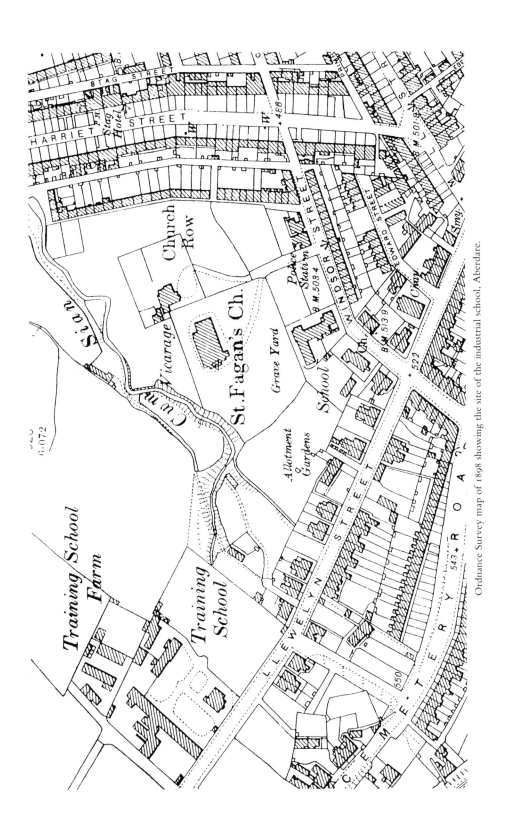

Ordnance Survey map of 1898 showing the site of the industrial school, Aberdare.

once the farm attached to the school was properly organised (Hosp. & Trng. Sch. Comm. Min. Bk. 7 May 1880).

A shoemaker appointed to teach the boys that craft was very successful. He showed a profit of £78 17s.0d. for the half-year ending September 1880, and so many shoes were made that they were advertised for sale in *The Western Mail* in November 1881. A tailor was appointed in 1880 to give the boys training, and he also made a profit. The Board of Guardians then bought a set of brass band instruments and engaged a trainer twice a week for two-hour music sessions.

Less interest was shown in the academic education of the children, partly because the emphasis was placed upon enabling them to earn a living. The first order for books and stationery was submitted on 16 January 1880:

TABLE 16

'3 doz. Standard I Readers.
2½ doz. Standard II Readers.
1½ doz. Standard III Readers.
1 doz. Standard IV Readers.
1 set of Moffat's Arithmetic Test Cards B & C.
1 gross of double-lined Exercise Books.
1 gross of single-lined Exercise Books.
½ gross of Plain.
2 Black Boards.
2 Easels.
6 boxes of pens.
1½ doz. boxes of slate pencils.
2 boxes chalk.'
(Hosp. & Trng. Sch. Comm. Min. Bk. 16 Jan. 1880).

The eighteen hours of schooling they had each week yielded good results. Dr. Clutterbuck, who made an inspection in October 1878, was pleased with the number of passes; he considered the discipline excellent and the whole tone of the school much improved. Inspector Bircham reported in 1877 '*There is a marked improvement in the children since their removal from the workhouse. I should not know them to be the same children*'. At that time, there were 116 children in the school. He found the wards well-ventilated, food and bedding good, and the health of the children improved. They were sent out for 'recreation' to Aberdare Park nearby, twice a week.

After it had been open for three years, the Superintendent reviewed its progress (Hosp. & Trng. Sch. Comm. Min. Bk. 4 June 1880). During that period, 65 orphans, 125 deserted children and 220 with mothers and fathers in the workhouse had passed through the school. It was the third category which proved most difficult because some of the parents were in the habit of taking them out for a month or a fortnight. During this time, old haunts of vice were revisited where they heard nothing but the vilest and most obscene language. They did not attend school during these periods and came back to Aberdare Industrial School morally and educationally damaged. Some children were sent to beg in the street so that their parents could live on the proceeds. In one instance, a mother had sent her little girl of six around public houses to sing obscene songs to obtain money. As far as the orphans were concerned, during the whole time they were at school they had no relatives or friends, and visiting days were blank for them. Yet when they were old enough to work, 'uncles' and 'aunts' appeared, anxious to know them. When girls were sent to service, these so-called relatives and friends visited them and interfered until eventually the girls absconded or were asked to leave. Applicants for children usually asked whether they had any relatives living before engaging them. Over three years, out of 19 girls sent to domestic service, six absconded due to interference and the other 13 worked well. The superintendent began the practice of visiting children after they had left the Industrial School. He found it surprising and pleasing to see their faces brightening when he called on them, and he believed that they were glad to know that even after leaving, they were not entirely forgotten. He added that the Board of Guardians took an interest in them and welcomed reports on them.

The educational progress of the children was further praised by Dr. Clutterbuck in 1883. The total number of children at the school was 131, of

> The following Report appeared in The Visitors Report Book viz
>
> 11th April 1882.
>
> Visited the School in all its departments, and was delighted to find everywhere proof of order, discipline and judicious kindness. As a Ratepayer, I feel grateful to those who founded this Excellent Institution on so sound a basis, and who secured for its such excellent superintendence.
>
> (Signed)   Aberdare
>
> I was accompanied by Mr Albert Rutson who was as much pleased as I was
>
> "A"

Lord Aberdare's entry in the Industrial School Visitor's Book.

whom 101 were examined; 99 passed in reading, 97 in writing and 97 in arithmetic. The Inspector considered the school was gaining so much success that small prizes should be considered (Minutes MTBG, 22 Sep. 1883). One visitor of note on 11 April 1882 was H. A. Bruce, now Lord Aberdare, who entered the following comment in the Visitors' Book: '*Visited the school in all its departments, and was delighted to find everywhere proof of order, discipline and judicious kindness. As a ratepayer, I feel grateful to those who founded this excellent institution on so sound a basis, and who secured for it such excellent superintendence*'. (Hosp. & Trng. Sch. Comm. Min. Bk. 21 April 1882). For Lord Aberdare, it was the realisation of a long-cherished aim, even though it was Rees H. Rhys who was instrumental in bringing it to fruition.

THE SICK

Another category of paupers for whom it was difficult to provide adequate facilities within the workhouse was the sick, for whom the barest provision was made. The Poor Law Board made no attempt to interfere with the usual practice of granting outdoor relief, but the Local Government Board after 1871 adopted a sterner approach. Writing in January 1870 to the Poor Law Board, the Clerk to Merthyr Tydfil Board of Guardians outlined the policy adopted towards them (PRO MH12/16334, 15 Jan. 1870). As a rule, no sick pauper was ordered into the workhouse unless he/she was suspected of pretending to be ill. The nature of each case was considered, conditions such as syphilis, itch and pregnancy being ordered inside. Lunatics were brought to the workhouse prior to removal to an asylum. Old people were usually asked whether they wanted to be admitted; some of them in poor lodgings often preferred the workhouse infirmary.

Most infirmaries were grim places with blank, white-washed walls, brick or stone floors without any covering, the only furniture being beds and a few chairs. Arrangements for washing the sick and keeping the wards clean were usually unsatisfactory. The quality of nursing was invariably poor and the practice of using male and female paupers for this purpose was thoroughly bad. As payment, the latter usually received allowances of gin or beer, sometimes with unfortunate consequences. (Longmate, 1974, p. 210).

Deaths in workhouses, under inhuman conditions, led to a national inquiry commissioned by *The Lancet* in 1865, and the formation of 'An Association for Improving the condition of the Sick Poor'. The publication of reports on workhouse infirmaries led to public discussion and parliamentary debates and the Poor Law Board sent out letters urging boards of guardians to spend what was necessary on sick paupers who were not to be subject to deterrent conditions.

In the workhouse in Merthyr Tydfil Union the accommodation consisted of four men's rooms, one fever ward, one recovery room, four women's rooms, one 'lying-in' ward and a recovery room for women, sufficient, in total, for 65 people. The staff consisted of one house surgeon, a nurse and an assistant. Since there was no public hospital, except after 1870, an Infectious Diseases Hospital, it was believed that a greater number of serious cases was admitted to this

The workhouse from the cholera graveyard, showing the infirmary building on the left.

infirmary than in any other town of the same population in the United Kingdom (PRO MH12/16333, 28 Jan. 1865).

The serious nature of some cases in the Infirmary is shown by the following request by the workhouse surgeon:

> '*I take this opportunity of mentioning the case of Thomas Barker admitted to the Infirmary about a week ago. Eighteen months since he had his thigh amputated, but in consequence of disease of the stump it is necessary to enable him to work to have amputation performed again. Mr. Dyke has seen him and concurs with me in the necessity for the operation and I should feel obliged by your deciding whether I shall be entitled to any fee for its performance. In a similar case I believe my predecessor had a fee allowed.*
> *Signed,* Francis Allday.'   (Minutes MTBG, 10 Oct. 1863).

The workhouse infirmary had, in fact, become the poor man's hospital. Between 1 June 1863 and 1 June 1864, the house surgeon treated 557 patients in the infirmary, exclusive of inmates suffering from slight illness. In the six months ending 30 September 1864, 268 cases were treated by this officer who also looked after the two nurseries and the idiot ward. When infectious diseases broke out among the children, the only place to put them was in the attics of the workhouse. The house surgeon made daily visits to the infirmary wards, sometimes attending three or four times a day to urgent cases and even calling on Sunday. A dispenser was employed three hours a day for the needs of pauper patients.

The inadequate nature of the workhouse infirmary was put to the test in 1865 when there were four epidemics : measles, scarlet fever, smallpox and typhus. In April and May 1865, smallpox and typhus caused havoc and conditions in the infirmary were described as 'chaotic' (PRO MH12/16333, 5 May 1865). Out of 71 cases of typhus, 11 were fatal. Both nurses and the women taken from the workhouse to look after patients were taken ill. At one stage, there were between 70 and 80 patients in the infirmary and only with difficulty was a ward set aside for female patients. The fever wards were in contact with the rest of the building and were totally inadequate. The employment of paupers as nurses was most unsatisfactory as they had less resistance to disease than people who were better nourished. These problems were outlined in Dr. Allday's Report:

> '*I beg to forward for your considration the following Report on the Fever at the Infirmary in the year 1865.*
>
> *The number of cases of Typhus and Typhoid was 71: of these 38 were imported from the Town, and 33 took the disease from those brought in. The number of fatal cases, including three pauper nurses, was 11. Both the paid nurses and all the women taken from the House to attend on patients suffering with fever were attacked. The accommodation for this class of disease at the Infirmary is very defective.*'

(Minutes MTBG, 6 April 1866).

In 1866, great improvements took place in the workhouse infirmary. Extensive alterations were carried out, the fever wards were improved, new closets were installed and deal floors replaced the stone paving in the wards (PRO MH12/16333, 19 May 1866). In July 1867, Inspector Graves reported that there was ample accommodation not only for the ordinary sick, but also for foul [venereal diseases] and fever cases. Four rooms, two large and two small, had been added, with two paid nurses to attend the patients. He considered the new additions to be the best part of what was originally a badly-constructed building (PRO MH12/16333, 13 July 1867).

Despite these improvements, by October 1872, the infirmary was described as '*altogether inadequate for the needs of so large a Union*' (PRO MH12/16335, 29 Oct. 1872). No proper classification of the sick was posssible, so that Inspector Davy found the infectious wards full of the ordinary sick as well as a woman recovering from fever. In a ward of five beds, there was one particularly foul case which should have been segregated from the rest, but the workhouse surgeon stated that nothing could be done because of shortage of space. The wards were not as clean as they should have been, and the head nurse could neither read nor write. The buildings were damp owing to an adjoining spring, and the drainage was bad. Since the infirmary had been connected to the drainage system of the town, there had been a regurgitation of sewer gases and a plague of rats. Cases of infectious diseases had to be carried up a common staircase which raised the question of whether they should have been admitted at all under such circumstances.

At first, the Board of Guardians refused to admit that there was anything wrong with the infirmary. While conceding that rats had eaten wood in the corridors, they thought it could be easily remedied. However, they must have been more worried than they admitted because they called in the surveyor of the Local Board of Health to report on its sanitary condition (Minutes MTBG, 19 June 1875). He stated that the floors of the dormitories were decaying rapidly and recommended that new concrete floors should be laid after 6 inches of clay beneath had been removed. The drainage system also needed ventilation to relieve the pressure of gas. This work was carried out immediately, and by 21 August 1875, the infirmary was described as '*very clean, sweet and tidy*' and ready to receive patients. It was decided not to enlarge it because a separate hospital was being built in Aberdare and the burden on the rates would be too great at a time of severe industrial depression.

The project of building a hospital at Aberdare had first been considered in 1870 (Minutes MTBG, 18 June 1870). The infirmary at Merthyr Tydfil was too small for the needs of the whole Union, while Aberdare district, containing a population of 40,000, had no public hospital at all. It was seven miles distant from Merthyr Tydfil, being separated by a range of hills. Most of the sick people in Aberdare had to be treated in their own homes because of the difficulty of conveying them to the workhouse infirmary. Consequently, an application was made to the Poor Law Board for sanction to build a hospital for 40 people at a cost of £3,500. This was granted, even though it was considered exceptional to provide a separate infirmary (PRO MH12/16334, 18 June 1870). Not until January 1875 was it completed, at a cost of £6,586. From the outset, it was doomed to failure, for whereas it was designed to accommodate 53 patients, it rarely had more than 26, the average being 18, at a cost of £40 per annum per patient. Most of patients had chronic complaints which could have been treated in the workhouse (PRO MH12/16337, 20 April 1876). Men injured in colliery accidents refused to enter the hospital, preferring to remain in their own homes. The building itself had serious constructional problems, the infectious wards being in the wrong position and incapable of isolation. Housing the officers at a distance from the wards had produced problems of control and irregularities of behaviour. With all these drawbacks, Inspector Mowat of the Local Government Board concluded that nothing could be done to make it a good infirmary. The Board of Guardians consequently decided to convert it into an industrial school and were congratulated by the Local Government Board on this decision.

TABLE 17

SYPHILIS CASES		
Years	Males	Females
1882	7	31
1883	6	29
1884	17	15

(Minutes MTBG, 31 May 1884).

Owing to the closure of Aberdare hospital, improvements in the workhouse infirmary once more became a pressing necessity. By February 1878, it was accommodating 60 patients with a further 77 under treatment in various parts of the workhouse (PRO MH12/16338, 12 Feb. 1878). There was general need for improvement in the wards for the old and infirm, and throughout the infirmary. A syphilis ward was built in 1885 for the increased number of cases.

The infirmary remained unsatisfactory, with the result that when Inspector Fuller visited it in 1893, he could only find praise for the mortuary which he described as a good one (PRO MH12, 18 May 1893). Inspector Bircham in November of that year said that the only solution was to build a new infirmary and use the existing one for imbeciles and non-acute sick (PRO MH12/16349, 9 Nov. 1893).

At one stage, one nurse and a pauper assistant were responsible for 137 patients and even when an extra nurse was considered, only a probationer could be obtained. Inspector Fuller, writing in May 1893, pointed out that 40-50 serious surgical cases requiring skilled nursing were dealt with in the infirmary during the course of a year, yet the head nurse had no surgical training as she was a midwife, and the two probationers who helped could not take responsibility for serious cases. He believed that patients had died who could have been saved with the services of a good, trained, surgical nurse (PRO MH12/16349, 18 May 1893). The head nurse not only looked after 80 chronic and acute cases, but also saw to the venereal wards. During the night-time there was no nurse on duty at all. It was a damning indictment that conditions which had been bitterly criticised in *The Lancet* Inquiry in 1865, were still prevalent thirty years later in the Merthyr Tydfil Union.

THE ABLE-BODIED

As we have seen from background legislation, the relief of able-bodied paupers inside the workhouse which should have been one of the most important functions of this institution, failed to have much influence on the very category against which it was directed. Few of them accepted indoor relief, even in times of extreme hardship. During the bitter strike and lock-out of 1875, Inspector Bircham reported on 30 March that there were only 21 able-bodied paupers in the workhouse as compared with 11 in the same period of the previous year, (PRO MH12/16337, of the same date). This was partly due to the fear and hatred with which the workhouse was regarded, partly to the way the unemployed managed to survive on credit and also to the expedients resorted to by the Board of Guardians to curtail relief to this class during the prolonged strike of 1875 (see Chapter 9).

When the able-bodied and their families had to enter the workhouse, they were categorised according to age and sex. Husbands, wives and children were separated. Able-bodied adults had to do task work, and consequently stone-breaking, hand-grinding and oakum-picking were provided. Wood-cutting was also introduced after 1870. The task work done in workhouses was meant to be a deterrent to the able-bodied and for that reason it was irksome and penal in character. Women and girls did housework and, when there was a shortage

The side entrance to the workhouse.

of such workers, it was not unusual for outdoor, able-bodied, female paupers to be ordered to work in the workhouse for a number of days each week while still remaining on outdoor relief. Thus in 1880, female outdoor paupers were ordered to work in the laundry at the workhouse for 6d a day and officers' rations (Minutes MTBG, 8 May 1880). When the master of the workhouse complained that he was short of domestic help, the Guardians ordered the relieving officers to send able-bodied women with two children to work in the workhouse three days a week in return for wages, food and outdoor relief (Minutes MTBG, 12 May 1883).

Apart from the provision of task work, Merthyr Tydfil Board of Guardians showed little interest, except in times of crisis, when they had to admit paupers in this class. They showed more concern when discharging them. To assist them until they obtained work, small sums of one or two shillings were granted, much to the annoyance of the Poor Law Board which tried to discontinue the practice (PRO MH12/16331, 22 June 1861). Inspector Graves pointed out that able-bodied paupers should not be released unless there was a reasonable chance of obtaining work at once, otherwise the money could be misused. In spite of his advice the Board of Guardians continued payment so that a person discharged could have food and lodging while searching for work. It was later changed to granting bread and cheese for the first day of the discharge, but the Guardians refused to abandon the practice, despite opposition from the Local Government Board.

Most able-bodied paupers were only too glad to leave the workhouse as soon as possible because the regime was so unbearably harsh. Corn-grinding, stone-breaking and oakum-picking were monotonous and painful tasks which no one would endure for a day longer than could be helped. The domestic work given to women was hard labour which often amounted to nine hours a day of back-breaking, exhausting work. Prison would have been an easier mode of life for these unfortunate people whose only crime was poverty.

Dowlais from the cinder-heaps. *The Illustrated London News*, 1875.

CHAPTER 9

The Able-bodied outside the Workhouse, 1853-1894

The problem of able-bodied pauperism was everywhere the most difficult to tackle. It became acute during periods of economic depression and industrial strife when the workhouse test was totally inadequate. The Board of Guardians knew at such times that it was impossible to refuse masses of people outdoor relief without running the risk of serious disturbances or possible riots. They also learned that it was far more expensive to maintain families in the workhouse than to give them outdoor relief to tide them over.

The period 1850-1873, described as the great mid-Victorian boom, was one of uneven industrial development. In the 1850, there were 165 furnaces in blast in Wales producing almost a million tons of pig-iron out of a total of 3,600,000 tons for the whole of Britain. But the search for new processes led to the replacement of iron by steel, and, at Dowlais, Bessemer steel was used almost

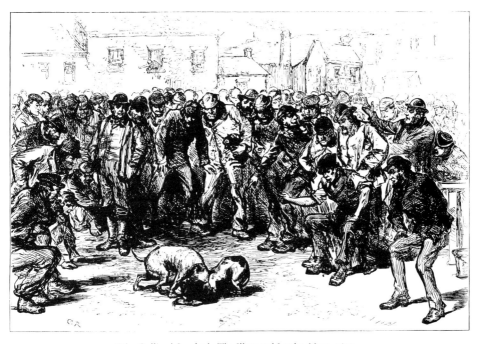

'The Colliers' Sunday'. *The Illustrated London News*, 1873.

exclusively for the manufacture of steel rails. As the cost of setting up the necessary plant for the production of steel was often prohibitive, the result was that one ironworks after another closed down. In November 1858, there was great depression in the iron trade in the Aberdare Valley. Ironmasters in Merthyr Tydfil also complained of lack of orders and tried to delay completion of tasks so as not to put men out of work. Large customers refused all rails not delivered according to contract in the hope of buying later on cheaper terms. Penydarren Works stopped in 1858, Hirwaun Works in 1859, and the Dowlais Works discharged 200-300 men at the end of 1859. In the opinion of the local press, '*All these facts taken together weighed heavily on the humbler classes and tended to augment the mass of pauperism already existing*' (*CMG*, 19 Nov. 1859).

As the iron industry came to be regarded as obsolete, the sale coal industry expanded:

TABLE 18

PARISH OF ABERDARE
COAL OUTPUT IN 000's OF TONS

YEAR	OUTPUT
1844	177
1845	193
1849	434
1850	477
1854	1,009
1855	1,204
1859	1,633
1860	1,755
1864	2,048
1865	1,976
1869	2,142
1870	2,071
1874	1,963

(Morris and Williams, 1958, p. 108).

Broadly speaking, the years 1873-1894 were characterised by economic depression. The period 1874-1877 was marked by a lack of growth or slowly rising levels of production. Between 1877 and 1879, almost all branches of trade were depressed and unemployment rose to its highest level in the fifty years before the 1914-1918 war. The depression in the South Wales coal trade was accompanied by wage cuts and strikes which caused Merthyr Tydfil Board of Guardians great problems.

Throughout the period under review, colliers and ironworkers were susceptible to the effects of the trade cycle, with the result that they lived almost always on the verge of poverty. (See Appendices 9-12). In addition, wages were low for long hours of dangerous, heavy work, so it is understandable that there should grow up a sense of 'outraged justice' (Jones, 1987, pp. 105-138). This is shown when, in 1857, a 15% wage cut for colliers in the Aberdare Valley brought 4,000-5,000 men out on strike in December. The cut was introduced by concerted action on the part of the coal-owners and without any consultation with the men. Professor Jones points out that the strike was not only about wages, it was about industrial relations and social attitudes. The men complained of being treated like animals: *We felt, standing there in the market place, like animals driven forth at the behest of and for the satisfaction of the masters'* (Jones, 1966, p. 44).

The *Cardiff and Merthyr Guardian* commented on the prevailing attitude towards trade unions (combinations) and showed the great bitterness which characterised industrial disputes:

> '*THE IRON AND COAL DISTRICTS OF GLAMORGANSHIRE*
> *The strike at Aberdare does not appear likely to terminate as soon as was hoped. In one or two pits the men, who last week returned to work, have again turned out, and intimidation is used to prevent those from working who would be glad to do so. Some strangers have been brought from a distance, but their advent is regarded with great hatred by the colliers, who hoot at them, and fix threatening notices to their doors'* (CMG 2 Jan. 1858).

The strike lasted for seven weeks and the situation became so desperate that troops had to be called in to maintain order. Through sheer necessity and semi-starvation, the men were forced back by the beginning of February 1858, having to accept a further 5% reduction to compensate the owners for their losses during the strike. This strike was better organised than previous stoppages; colliers at work provided subscriptions to support those out of work. The increase in the volume of pauperism in Aberdare parish was shown as follows:

TABLE 19

ABERDARE PARISH

Half Year Ending	Indoor	Outdoor
March 1857	38	886
March 1858	60	1,064

(Merthyr Tydfil Union Abstracts).

The Board of Guardians were not very concerned about the strike, the only reference in their minutes being general advice about how to deal with increased applications in the approaching winter months (Minutes MTBG, 14 Nov. 1857). Most of the strikers must have managed on charity, and possibly on what they had from their various Friendly Societies, as well as credit from shopkeepers. Poor relief was a last resort.

During the trade crisis in 1865, there was a cut-back in coal production in Aberdare which, coupled with the decline of the iron industry, meant an increase in pauperism. The Board of Guardians decided to deal with this by sending all indoor Irish paupers back to Ireland, making task work for able-bodied men in the workhouse harder in respect of stone-breaking, and imposing the workhouse test on all able-bodied women with one child (Minutes MTBG, 24 June 1865). The measure seems to have been effective because there was an increase in the number of indoor paupers and a decrease in the outdoor paupers for the half year ending September 1865.

In 1871, the Poor Law Board was replaced by the Local Government Board which was more zealous in its attack on outdoor relief and more confident in its dealings with the Boards of Guardians. As respresentatives of the propertied interests, the Guardians sought to keep down rates regardless of personal suffering. Their concern was with the moral character of destitute people, for they believed that everyone could by thrift prepare for bad times. While outdoor relief was not and could not be abolished, the number of outdoor paupers declined. The offer of the workhouse in every kind of economic weather led to the same result—people got along without it.

Fear of the workhouse was shown by this report in the *Merthyr Express*:

'*Merthyr Board of Guardians*
What has become of them?

Dr. James remarked that a short time ago the Board had passed a resolution to visit all the paupers in the Union; now he would like to know what had become of those 19 who were ordered in by the Board last Saturday but had not come in; had

Tip girls at the Dowlais Ironworks. *The Illustrated London News*, 1873.

they been left to starve, or what? It struck him that out of the 19 some would surely be in actual want, and he thought it would be a very proper thing to visit them and find out what became of them.'
(*ME* 20 July 1872).

In the 1870s, as a trade recession set in, industrial unrest increased. The strike which started in South Wales on 1 June 1871, was against a 5% wage reduction imposed by the sale-coal colliery owners. It was a test both of the Amalgamated Association of Miners and the Association of Steam-colliery Owners. It brought no severe burden on the rates because the miners were able to obtain work at the pits owned by the ironmasters (Williams & Morris, op. cit., p. 278). The amount of strike-pay each miner received for 12 weeks totalled only £1 5s.7d., hardly sufficient to keep them or their families off the rates. The AAM came out of the strike with enhanced prestige having not only secured an increase of 2½% in wages, but having fought off the threat of black-leg labour. The Trade Union Act of 1871 gave trade unions the recognition, rights and protection they needed.

After this strike there was a period of uneasy peace before the next strike in 1873 when the ironmasters demanded a 10% reduction in wages which was resisted by their colliers who came out on strike on 1 January 1873. The fact that the sale-coal collieries continued to work enabled the AAM to pay those on strike 10/- a week. When strikers at Pontlottyn in the parish of Gelligaer applied

Conference between ironmasters and workmen's delegates at Cardiff, 1873. *The Illustrated London News.*

for poor relief, the Board of Guardians set up a local committee to organise stone-breaking (Minutes MTBG, 18 Jan. 1873). Two dozen hammers and rings were ordered, but, fortunately, Rhymney Ironworks offered work to some strikers.

> 'We [the Gelligaer task work committee] visited Pontlottyn on Monday last and from the R. officer of Gelligaer that there were very few fresh applications for relief, and that Limestone breaking would not be required.
>
> We then called upon Mr. Laybourne the Manager of the Rhymney Iron Works and got from him what the Co. were actually doing for men who were out of work. We find from his statement that they were employing 170 men from Pontlottyn paying them 1/- for about 5 hours time.
>
> We also find that the Rhymney Works are still carrying on 7 Blast Furnaces which must employ a great number of hands, and we believe that the poverty of the place is not so great as represented on Saturday last. Mr. Laybourne has promised that should the Board of Guardians still wish to carry out the Limestone breaking, he is prepared to deliver stone at the Road side Pond at 3/6 per Ton.
>
> We have ordered about 2 Dozen Hammers and rings ready should many applications be made this day, but as yet we have not ordered any Limestone on the ground.
>
> Your Committee are of opinion that with the information they received think it rather premature to move further in the matter for the present.'
> (Minutes MTBG, 25 Jan. 1873).

There was a great deal of suffering among ironworkers at Dowlais, Cyfarthfa and Aberdare, where soup kitchens were organised for women and children. The workhouse test was applied with little effect; on 1 March 1873, 46 able-bodied applicants were ordered into the workhouse but not one complied (CMG 8 March 1873). Most strikers preferred to live on credit given by shopkeepers, and if that was not available and strike pay was insufficient, they went about begging. On 22 March 1873, *The Cardiff and Merthyr Guardian* reported, 'After 11 weeks of idleness and semi-starvation, the men returned to work'. The settlement whereby the wage rates of December 1872 were restored was a substantial victory for the workmen, who had imposed no extra burden on the poor rates.

By this time, relationships between masters and men were full of hatred and distrust. As mines got deeper, they became more dangerous; explosions resulted in loss of lives, and falls of rock produced horrible accidents. Thus a strike in 1867 had been mainly concerned about safety and conditions of work. Workmen regarded their masters as oppressors and began questioning a system which made the rich richer and the poor poorer, when all they wanted was to ensure a minimum standard of living for workers.

On 1 January 1875 the men struck against a wage reduction of 10% for colliers. This time the AAM was ill-equipped for a long-fought battle of five months. The coal producers had combined to present a united front and included the most important iron and coal companies which together determined 70% of the output of the South Wales coalfield (Morris &

The Strike in South Wales. Exodus of miners from Merthyr Tydfil, 1873. *The Illustrated London News.*

Williams, p. 282). This strike tested the Board of Guardians to their limits and showed the intransigent nature of the New Poor Law at its worst. The ferocity of this dispute produced a debate which has never been settled, viz. whether public authorities should give poor relief to strikers whose unemployment was, in a sense, voluntary.

The provision of task work for the able-bodied on a sufficiently large scale became the main problem facing the Guardians, and the measures to deal with it became increasingly harsh as the strike deepened. On 30 January 1875, the Outdoor Labour Test Committee was set up. Its policy was to grant poor relief only to heads of families and to single men with families dependent on them (Minutes MTBG, 6 Feb. 1875). In return, stone-breaking had to be done at the following rates : limestone 1/- per cubic yard, field or quarry stone 1/4d per cubic yard. Stones had to be broken to a gauge of $2\frac{1}{4}$ inches, stones and rings being provided by the Board of Guardians. If sufficient stone could not be provided, men were to be employed at quarries. Relieving officers were ordered to communicate with the highway authorities to whom applicants for relief were to be sent, and District Committees in each area were to enforce these regulations. Where more than 20 men in a district were employed, a superintendent of labour was appointed. During the week ending 12 February 1875, the clerk to the Guardians reported that 1,500 able-bodied men had been given poor relief (PRO MH12/16337, 12 Feb. 1875).

By that time, the owners had decided on a 'lock-out' to prevent strikers being supported by men who remained at work. There was such great distress in the districts of Upper and Lower Merthyr Tydfil that both relieving officers broke down with exhaustion. Five hundred men in Gelligaer parish applied for relief and were given work by the Highway Board, for which they received payment half in money and half in food notes (Minutes MTBG 13 Feb. 1875).

The situation was so serious from 19 February onwards, that the Guardians met almost daily and it was decided that all single men should in future be relieved within the workhouse only.

> 'Resolved that in view of the possibility of the weather becoming so severe as to prevent men working in the open the committees are requested to provide sheds & if necessary to construct them. . .
> Resolved that all single men without encumbrance be relieved indoors as long as there's room in the house.
> . . . Resolved That the relief to the stonebreakers be given twice a week, one half in kind and other half in money
> Ordered that the notes for food be addressed generally so that they be taken to any shop.'
> (Minutes MTBG, 19 Feb. 1875).

An organised 'run' on the poor rates was attempted by the able-bodied and there was fear of a breach of the peace. On 25 February 1875 a secret meeting of the employers was held in London to discuss the matter. G. T. Clark (Chairman of the Board of Guardians and Trustee of the Dowlais Works), was present and it was decided to adopt 'the same uncompromising, silent resistance as heretofore'.

Richard Fothergill wrote to his lawyer W. Simons about it:

> 'Todays Meeting informal, Perfectly private, yet influentially attended the subject of the organized run on the poor rates & the general question very fully discussed with the result of the same uncompromising silent resistance in heretofore & no meeting of the Council.'
> (GRO D/D Xj, 25 Feb. 1875).

Such a meeting shows how the industrialists could not only present a united front as in the Association of Steam Coal Owners, but could use their influence behind the scenes to manipulate poor relief so as to starve out the strikers.

On 27 February 1875, 900 single, able-bodied men converged on the workhouse to force the Guardians to grant them poor relief. The master of the workhouse admitted as many as he could accommodate and then locked the doors. The rest drifted away leaving their comrades to wreck workhouse discipline (ME, 27 Feb. 1875). By 1 March, four of the able-bodied inmates had been expelled for insubordination and thereafter had to exist by their own means. By 13 March, it was necessary to install four policemen in the workhouse to maintain discipline (Minutes MTBG, 13 March 1875). All single men over 16 years were offered indoor relief only and men who were defiant in the stoneyards were ordered into the workhouse. Desperate for more task work, the Board of Guardians asked the Highway Board to take on men to build new roads.

Matters reached crisis point on 16 March 1875, when the Board of Guardians decided to take up an offer by the Dowlais Iron Company to provide work for

Richard Fothergill III.

Hensol Castle, enlarged by Rowland Fothergill in the 1840s. Lithograph by Hawkins, *circa* 1850.

25 able-bodied men at its collieries. If the strikers refused the work, they lost their poor relief, which meant they faced starvation, for there was no strike pay as the AAM funds were exhausted. In taking this line, the Guardians were in fact playing the masters' game, and it has to be remembered that Guardians and employers were in some cases the self-same men or were closely connected.

The cruel irony of offering men work in places where they had been locked out was given forceful expression on 16 March 1875, when a number of Cyfarthfa and Plymouth colliers appeared before the Guardians and were offered work at Dowlais Colliery.

> '*A number of Cyfarthfa and Plymouth Colliers having come down 8 were called in and appeared before the Board.*
> *They said that they were afraid to go to work at Dowlais in consequence of their having been informed that the work now offered to them had been refused by the Dowlais Colliers and therefore they would not work there.*
>
> *The Board having heard them at great length in reply stated that the Colliery at Dowlais was the only place where work was to be had at present & that the law left the Guardians no option but to refuse relief.*'
(Minutes MTBG, 16 March 1875).

George Thomas Clark.

Feeling ran so high that there was fear of a riot and extra policemen were drafted into Merthyr Tydfil.

The harshness and hypocrisy of the Guardians were revealed in the discussion on 17 March 1875 when Inspector Doyle of the Local Government Board attended the Guardians' meeting with a view to expounding a solution (*ME*, 20 March 1875). The Inspector put forward the resolution '*That the masters be asked whether they can give work to men out of employment at wages sufficient to keep them off the rates; and that they be asked to indicate the extent to which they would provide employment*'. If he had referred to the minutes of the Board of Guardians, he

William Menelaus.

would have known that such an offer had already been made. It is very likely that he did in fact know it, because he admitted that he was concerned purely with the provision of task work for the able-bodied, regardless of its consequences. With supreme irony, he urged the Guardians to observe an attitude of complete neutrality. He emphasised that they had no right to suggest the terms on which the men might be employed; they could only try to obtain work at wages sufficient to keep them off the rates, and refuse poor relief to those who would not accept this work. He considered that his resolution was based on an understanding of the position of the masters, the workmen and '*of a class which suffered through no fault of their own - the small ratepayers*'.

Not surprisingly, G. T. Clark, the chairman, gave his support, pointing out that they had already acted on this principle and would continue to do so. He promised that the Masters' Association would consider the request. One of the Guardians, Dr. J. W. James, was prepared to challenge the Inspector and Chairman. James was a member of the James faction, radical opponents of the ironmasters' autocracy in local and parliamentary politics. He was supported by another Guardian, W. Gould, who had been a Chartist. James asked whether the work to be offered was underground because, if so, the Guardians could be accused of supporting the masters against the men who would have to work at a 20% reduction of payment. He also questioned the right to refuse relief to men who would not accept such work. '*To refuse relief to 12,000-15,000 men simply because 25 were offered it and rejected it, was straining the law*'. The Inspector replied that when this task work was offered to each collier in turn, and they all refused, nothing could be done since it was not just 25 or 30 men who refused but all of them.

At this meeting, a deputation of colliers appeared before Inspector Doyle asking what they were to do as they had been stopped stone-breaking and their poor relief had been cut off. They admitted refusing work at Dowlais because they would have been branded as 'turn-coats'. The Inspector was adamant that the Guardians had no power to relieve them if they refused this work, whereupon the colliers offered to go to work *en masse*, but this was refused and it was pointed out that the Guardians had to be 'impartial'! When the men asked if they would have to starve if they did not go to work at Dowlais, the Inspector replied that it was not a matter of feeling but a point of law.

With an explosive situation on their hands, 12,000–15,000 men and their dependants all completely destitute and facing starvation, some action had to be taken. It took the form of even more stringent measures in respect of the able-bodied. Meeting on 19 March 1875, the Board of Guardians fixed the hours of work in the stoneyards as follows: 8 a.m. - 12 noon and 1 p.m. - 5 p.m. Relief would only be given to men who worked the whole time, every day of the week. Stone-breaking was extremely hard work requiring great strength; though men's hands blistered and bled handling such rough materials, they continued to work for fear of being dismissed for indiscipline. Men working on roads were given longer hours: 7.00 a,m, – 12 noon and 1 p.m. – 5 p.m. Even on Good Friday, which was regarded as the holiest day in the Christian calendar, men had to work in the stoneyards.

A pawn shop in Merthyr Tydfil, 1875. *The Illustrated London News.*

'Proposed by the Revd. W. Davies and seconded by Mr. J. W. James:
'*That the men do not work on Good Friday.*'
Amendment moved by Mr. Martin and seconded by Mr. R. Griffiths:
'*That the men do work on Friday. Amendment carried.*'
(Minutes MTBG, 25 March 1875).

The Superintendent of Relief reported that 71 men in the hospital stoneyard threw down their hammers at 11 a.m. that day and left saying that they were going to church. For that action they were dismissed and left destitute (*ME*, 3 April 1875).

Great controversy raged over a resolution adopted by the Board of Guardians on 20 March 1875 to the effect that in future all relief to the able-bodied was to be by way of a loan.

> "*Moved by Mr. Rees H. Rhys, Seconded by Mr. Llewellyn and Resolved*
> *That all relief to able bodied men whether stones be broken or not be in future by*
> *way of loan*
> *Moved by Mr. Wm. Gould, Seconded by Revd. W. Davies*
> *That when a man does actual work and receives relief to the amount of 6/- for*
> *breaking 4 yards of stones that he should not be called on to refund the money.*
> *Motion Carried.*'
> (Minutes MTBG, 20 March, 1875).

The proposer of this motion was Rees H. Rhys, a mineral agent and property owner in Aberdare, who had also been an agent to Fothergill, the ironmaster.

Waiting for relief outside the workhouse at Merthyr, 1875. *The Illustrated London News.*

He was supported by G. T. Clark on the grounds that it was necessary to distinguish between the deserving and the undeserving poor, and also to protect the ratepayers. This was challenged by the two Guardians, J. W. James and William Gould, who alleged that it was unfair to expect men to repay relief for which they had done task work; it amounted to double payment—work and money. Their amendment was defeated but they returned to the battle on 3 April 1875 when Gould said that '*He was ashamed to see such a resolution passed in what was called a Christian country*' (*ME*, 3 April 1875). The best result he could achieve was a promise that the Board of Guardians reserved the right of discretion in exercising repayment.

G. T. Clark expressed his views on the strike in letters to the *Merthyr Express*:

'*. . . It is true, as you state, that the iron trade has long been subject to great and frequent fluctuations, and the system of engagement "at call" between employer and employed has worked ill, because the employed have not yet acquired those habits of thrift without which true independence is possible. At present, the workmen who are most ready to precipitate a strike are young men who have saved nothing, who see no disgrace in putting their hands into their neighbours' pockets, and who, at the worst, can migrate; whereas the older and steadier men, who have saved money, and, in a large number of cases, are cottage owners, are like the masters, and for the same reasons, by no means prompt to act . . .*' (*ME*, 20 March 1875).

'*The teaching of the Unions is, practically that wages are fixed by the masters and that the men have only to be firm to obtain what they can desire.*

Of late years the great mass of men employed in the ironworks and collieries have been content to do as little work as possible and but too often have done that little in a slovenly manner. Many have left work upon the slightest excuse, or upon no excuse at all, and stayed away for days together regardless of the loss they thereby inflict upon the master, and ignorant of its reaction upon themselves. . . .' (*ME*, 3 April 1875).

Further efforts were made to obtain task work for the able-bodied. An agreement was made with Merthyr Tydfil Local Board of Health to employ 540 men on parish roads (Minutes MTBG, 19 March 1875). The rate of payment was 7/6d for a man and wife, 1/6d for each child under 6, though boys of 13-16 years would have to break stones in order to qualify for poor relief.

The offer by the owners of the Dowlais, Cyfarthfa and Plymouth Collieries to provide work for colliers at the wage rate prevailing in January 1870, was seized upon by the Board of Guardians (Minutes MTBG 3 April 1875). Sufficient work could be provided if two collieries were left open, the coal being stockpiled. Rates of payment were fixed at 5/- a week for a single man, 8/- a week for a married man without children, and 2/- a week for each child under 12 years of age. Able-bodied men on strike were to be given relief notes to go to the works from which they had been locked out, three days' work being sufficient to earn the equivalent in poor relief.

This measure produced a fierce discussion within the Board of Guardians. Rees H. Rhys pointed out that the offer of work by the Dowlais Company had

The lock-out in South Wales—miners breaking stones on the Brecon Road. Drawn by H. Johnson for *The Graphic*.

only come about after '*pressing representations*', and G. T. Clark emphasised that the Dowlais Company wished to be passive, '*having no desire to bring into collision capital and labour on one side, and poor relief on the other*' (*ME*, 24 April 1875). The question must be asked how it was possible for Clark to divorce his interests as a trustee of Dowlais Iron Company from his duties as Chairman of the Board of Guardians? Knowing full well how they interacted, how could he possibly claim neutrality? This was the test which broke the strike and forced the men to capitulate.

Dr. J. W. James attacked this offer of work as being a 'dodge'. Not only was relief being refused to colliers who would not accept work at these collieries, but to puddlers who were out of work through no fault of their own. He described their treatment as cruel and warned of the danger of desperate men swarming on the workhouse so that once it was full the Board of Guardians would have to give outdoor relief. In reply, G. T. Clark touched the heart of the matter when he replied that his concern was for the ratepayers. (He should also have added that his concern was for the employers). He regarded the 'pull' on the rates as enormous, falling on the middle-class who paid 1/6d or 2/- in the pound, instead of previously 1/- and he considered the Guardians had a duty to them as well as to the poor. He believed the masters' offer of work would

Sufferers from the strike in search of relief.

enable colliers to earn '*sufficient to keep their wives and children, not in affluence, but from want*'. He objected to the word 'dodge' and said that the Guardians were only carrying out the law. Whatever form of words was used by G. T. Clark and Dr. J. W. James respectively, the fact remained that the strikers were being starved into submission.

By 15 May 1875, their suffering was so extreme that the strikers had to give in. A settlement was not reached until 29 May, when they agreed to a $12\frac{1}{2}\%$ reduction in wages and the operation of a sliding scale. They returned to work feeling great bitterness towards their masters and with their trade union seriously weakened. It says a great deal for their self-control and discipline that they had not resorted to mass violence.

This strike had shown the inadequacy of a Poor Law based on principles laid down in 1834 and which had ignored the causes of poverty. It had also shown how the powerful interests of the ironmasters' and coal owners' autocracy could still dominate the administration of poor relief and also be used as a weapon against strikes. Legally, the Guardians may have been right, but in practical terms they made further reform of the Poor Law inevitable. The cost of relieving the able-bodied was summed up in Merthyr Tydfil alone as follows:

TABLE 20

ABLE-BODIED RELIEF

Half Year Ending	District	Amount
March 1875	Merthyr Lower	£1,174. 13. 1.
September 1875	Merthyr Lower	£1,311. 15. 8.
March 1875	Merthyr Upper	£2,672. 2. 7.
September 1875	Merthyr Upper	£2,990. 17. 5.
		£8,149. 8. 9.

(Merthyr Tydfil Union Abstracts, March and September, 1875).

The Board of Guardians took quick measures to dismiss extra officers, and to sell the stones they had amassed, albeit at reduced rates.

CHAPTER 10

The Sick, Lunatics, Aged and Vagrants, 1853–1894

Reference has already been made to the responsibility of Guardians for sick people who became destitute. Writing to the Poor Law Board in 1870, the clerk to Merthyr Tydfil Board of Guardians outlined the policy adopted (PRO MH12/16334, 15 Jan. 1870). As a rule, no sick pauper was ordered into the workhouse unless imposture was suspected, or such a person was being badly attended at home. The nature of each case was considered, those affected by accidents almost always being given relief outside. Lunatics, if unmanageable, were brought to the workhouse prior to removal to an asylum. Old people were usually consulted about whether they wished to enter the workhouse; many who had no children were often neglected in lodgings and were better off in the workhouse infirmary. The wishes of the family of a sick pauper were rarely considered. Those on outdoor relief were looked after by medical officers employed solely by the Board of Guardians. In addition to medical attendance, outdoor relief in kind was provided, and in time of serious illness, wines and spirits were given under strict instructions (Minutes MTBG, 2 Oct. 1869).

Vaccination was an important responsibility which the Board of Guardians discharged. The Vaccination Act of 1853 made it obligatory for parents to arrange for infants to be vaccinated within four months of their birth. It was justified by Sir John Simon on the ground that *the man who indulged in a preference for smallpox did so to the detriment and danger of his neighbour*. Unfortunately, this measure was ineffective because there were no provisions for its actual enforcement. Dr. J. Ludford White informed the Poor Law Board in 1854 that the objects of the Vaccination Act of 1853 were being defeated in Merthyr Tydfil because parents would not bring their children to be vaccinated before they were three months old (PRO MH12/16329, 18 March 1854). As one of the vaccination officers employed by Merthyr Tydfil Board of Guardians, he estimated that less than half the children born in his district since 1853 had been vaccinated, and he believed that the parents disregarded the notices served upon them when they registered their children.

The seriousness of this problem was realised when smallpox broke out in 1863. The inspector of vaccination then pointed out that in the smallpox epidemic of 1857–1858, the mortality rate in Merthyr Tydfil Union exceeded, in proportion to the population, that of every other union in the whole country (Minutes MTBG, 31 Oct. 1863). He wanted large numbers of unprotected children to be vaccinated and urged that parents should be prosecuted for neglecting their duty. With the reappearance of smallpox in 1871, the vaccination officers once again visited homes, issued orders and prosecuted where there was neglect. By slow and painful progress, this disease was gradually brought under control.

When cholera appeared in Merthyr Tydfil in 1854, the town was just as dirty and ill-prepared as it had been in 1849. As a result of a letter from Dr. T. J. Dyke, the Merthyr Tydfil Local Board of Health and the Board of Guardians met to consider the problem (*CMG* 15 Sep. 1854). They decided to co-operate in the removal of all nuisances; house-to-house visitations were to be made by visitors under the control of the Board of Guardians. On the advice of local doctors, it was decided not to remove accumulations of filth but to cover them and to use disinfectants. Men formerly engaged on the highways were employed to do this work. Owners of pig-styes were served with notices and such nuisances as stagnant water were dealt with.

Even in times of crisis, a great deal of squabbling went on among various interests. Whereas the Guardians for Merthyr Tydfil parish were keen to take action to control the disease, Guardians from the country districts complained *'it would provide more medical attention than was needed for pauper cases ... and that it would be wiser for each works to care for its sick employees'* (*CMG* 15 Sep. 1854). William Crawshay objected to the possibility of his medical staff being forced to neglect his own employees for the sake of pauper patients, whereas John Evans of Dowlais Works took the opposite view, and pointed out that the

From sketches of the lock-out in South Wales, an interior scene, 'Back of Plough, Dowlais'.

134

homes of men belonging to each works were scattered, not in one location. He believed the doctors were the best judges of how to arrange a scheme of medical relief. This view prevailed, and at a special meeting, the town was divided into districts, each doctor attending to pauper patients in the district allotted to him. The fees were 10/6d per cholera case and 3 guineas a week for medicine and attendance in cases of diarrhoea, which were met by the Merthyr Tydfil Union. An all-night dispensary was opened for the supply of free medicines, and 600 precautionary notices were printed in English and Welsh. To accommodate the survivors of stricken families a house of refuge was set up at Ffynnon Tydfil, at a cost of £231 8s.2d. The following resolutions were passed:

> 'Ordered that the Clerk write to the Rector and Churchwardens of Merthyr recommending that all persons dying of Cholera be buried by themselves under the East Wall of the Burial Ground and that graves be dug 10 feet deep if possible. . . . It being represented to this Board that Mr Evan Rees, Carpenter, has not a sufficient supply of Coffins Ordered that the Clerk write to him to put on more men.'

> 'Resolved that a House of Refuge be immediately erected upon the spot of ground belonging to the Parish at Ffynnon Tydfil and that the same be immediately walled in; and that Mr. Henry the Surveyor of the Board of Health be requested to afford his assistance in preparing a Plan of a Building, capable of holding a hundred persons, by Monday next, and Mr. Evan Rees be desired to make immediate preparations for erecting the Building.'
> (Minutes MTBG, 18 & 23 Sep. 1854).

Cholera continued its ravages, especially in the most densely populated parts of the town of Merthyr Tydfil. The number of deaths for the month of September was 148. Mostly Irish immigrants were affected, and by 13 October 1854, 25 out of every 30 victims were Irish men, women and children. By 20 October, the epidemic reached a crisis, the average mortality being 15 persons a day. Many cases proved fatal within a few hours, and the recovery rate was lower than in 1849. In all, there were 316 deaths in Merthyr Tydfil parish before the disease disappeared, leaving its toll in human lives and its expense on the rates for the Board of Guardians and the Local Board of Health to reflect upon.

The reappearance of cholera in 1866 led to concerted action by the Board of Guardians and the Local Boards of Health of Merthyr Tydfil and Aberdare. On this occasion, public reaction to an initiative taken by Dowlais Iron Company in the interests of its workers is of particular interest. Relationships between the Company and its workmen were not good at this time, consequently, when it attempted to relieve workers attacked by cholera in a temporary hospital, such help was rejected. G. T. Clark was mortified by the response to the Dowlais hospital he had set up, and resolved never to take action of that kind again (*ME*, 15 Sep. 1866). The Board of Guardians sympathised with him: '*That this Board having heard from the Chairman the excellent arrangements he had made at Dowlais in establishing a Hospital for Cholera Patients, and having furnished it with every requisite and having himself and family attended the same, this Board expresses its sympathy with him in the present trying position he has now been placed in, and the*

G. T. Clark's hospital at Dowlais.

Board cannot but regret that all his endeavours have been in vain, and they also thank him most cordially for all he has done' (Minutes MTBG, 8 Sep. 1866). Large meetings of colliers were held in which they declared that they did not want such a hospital, and that if it were continued, they would go on strike. Not only was the hospital rejected, but the schools provided by the Company were closed as the workmen *'wished to manage their own educational affairs without interference from the Company'*. G. T. Clark did not appreciate the hatred and distrust that was developing between employer and employee, and failed to understand the resentment that his paternalism produced.

Public hostility was also demonstrated towards the activities of the Local Board of Health and of the Board of Guardians. The house-to-house visitations by doctors had caused considerable alarm, and they met with great hostility when they ordered the burning of soiled clothing and the compulsory disinfection of clothing. The practice of paying doctors' fees by the case, i.e. for each patient, also created opposition, as people thought it put a premium on killing (*ME* 22 Sep. 1866). So deep was the gulf between patients and doctors that the patients in hospitals refused to swallow medicines in case they died. The myth had gained ground that doctors 'meant to slay people with cholera'. Such prejudice showed how much education in public health remained to be done.

The atrocious suffering of the labouring masses made Merthyr Tydfil a legend as a town and a place to be feared. The first victim of cholera died on 24 August 1866, and the last on 20 October 1866.

The Board of Guardians took prompt action in this epidemic:

> '   *The Clerk to write to the Clerks of the Burial Boards drawing their attention to the 24 hours notice of burial and to suggest that the rule be abrogated for the present.*
>
> *The Clerk to write to John Gabe the Coffin contractor to keep a supply of Coffins ready, and that they be well pitched inside, for which an allowance will be made.*
>
> *Ordered that the Clerk write to the Catholic Priests of Dowlais and George Town to inform them of the necessity of speedy interment, and that no wakes will be allowed*'

(Minutes Cholera Committee minute book MTBG, 25 Aug. 1866).

> '*Mr. Cresswell attended and reported that a corpse lay at No 1 Flag & Castle Court Dowlais which it was expedient should be buried today.*
>
> *Ordered that the corpse be buried today, but if not practicable that the living be removed, and the house locked up, and that the house be disinfected and cleaned.*
>
> *Ordered that the clothes be burnt in the above case, and also in the case of a person dead of cholera at No 7 Cwm Canol Street Dowlais. Relieving Officer Wm. J. Jones to carry out these orders with the aid of the Police.*'

(Minutes Cholera Committee minute book, MTBG, 25 Aug. 1866).

> '*Ordered that James Westall town porter be employed to disinfect - burn clothes and put bodies in coffins at the following rate of wages viz.*
>
> *Handling wages of 20/- per week*
> *and for every body coffined   1/-*
> *   for every disinfecting   1/-*
> *   for every clothes burning   1/-*
>
> *Ordered a supply of disinfectant, to be kept at the Police Stations and at the Workhouse.*'

(Minutes Cholera Committee minute book, MTBG, 27 Aug. 1866)

During the epidemic, 275 people in Merthyr and Dowlais were attacked by cholera in its most virulent form and no fewer than 115 died. The number of choleraic diarrhoea cases during the same period was 1,819 of which 12 were fatal, bringing the total number of deaths to 127. In this epidemic, one in 26 in Merthyr Tydfil was attacked and one in 440 died.

The *Merthyr Express* referred to the suffering caused at Aberdare at this time:

Widowhood. From *Street Views* by John Thomson, 1877.

'The Cholera

New cases of cholera continue to occur in this district and very painful incidents in connection with sudden and unexpected deaths from the disorder crop up daily. Two little children - infants - have been removed to the public hospital in Gadlys-road in consequence of the death of their widowed mother. They are carefully looked after and the forlorn position of the poor little things attracts the attention of all who have business to visit the place; so much so that it is very likely now they have more friends than they ever had before. The man who has been carrying out the disagreeable duty of attending to the bodies and clothing of the victims is laid up with the disease and no end of difficulty is experienced in getting a person to perform his work. The disfavour with which men employed are looked upon by the ignorant, contributes more towards the difficulty of getting the posts filled than the disagreeableness of the work to be performed. This week one of the sanitary inspectors received an unstamped letter bearing the Cardiff postmark and addressed to him as a "body-scratcher" ... The hospital is being made continual use of ... and will doubtless prove a blessing to the place.'
(*ME* 22 Sep. 1866).

Looking for the causes of this outbreak, a writer in *The Merthyr Express* stated that the town of Merthyr Tydfil suffered from two great evils: the lack of privy accommodation and overflowing cesspools. In the first respect, it was alleged that no town in England could equal Merthyr Tydfil; the only fair comparison would be an Indian town. Of necessity, cesspools had to be tolerated until the sewage works were completed, but some action had to be taken in the mean-time to clean them out (*ME* 3 Nov. 1866). Summing up the expenses of paying doctors, refitting the hospital, compensating for burnt clothing and bedding, using tons of lime as disinfectant, engaging extra sanitary inspectors, digging graves and providing hearses, the editor stated, '*It behoves the ratepayers of Merthyr Tydfil, for the sake of their pockets, apart from their humanity and good sense, to extirpate the causes of such pestilence*'.

Typhus and typhoid fever appeared in Dowlais in 1868 and continued to spread throughout 1869 and 1870. True typhus fever was characterised by high fever, delirium, crisis and a blotchy rash, and was often fatal. It was transmitted by the bite of the body louse but was most prevalent when malnutrition and squalid living conditions existed, as in Merthyr Tydfil. At this time, the distinction between typhus and typhoid was not properly understood. Typhoid fever was one of the enteric group of diseases caused mainly by a contaminated water supply. Water-borne diseases were found wherever people shared a contaminated water supply and there was a lack of proper sanitary facilities for the disposal of sewage. Owing to the lack of hospital accommodation, the sick were nursed at home. The Board of Guardians reopened the refuge at Tydfil's Well for the accommodation of healthy members of stricken families. In 1869, 402 cases of typhus were reported, and on the advice of Dr. T. J. Dyke, the refuge was converted into a fever hospital. The sewering of the area which was being undertaken by Merthyr Tydfil Local Board of Health at the time proved to be the best long-term preventative measure against disease.

'Relapsing fever' or 'famine fever' appeared in November 1870 (PRO MH12/16334, 25 Nov. 1870). The outbreak was traced to a vagrant who arrived in Merthyr Tydfil from Tredegar where it had been epidemic. Another case came from Maesteg; the man concerned infected the family with whom he lodged and also two women sent to nurse them. Twenty-three tramps had the fever between October 1870 and January 1871. They were removed from the common lodging houses to a hospital, their clothes were fumigated and the places where they stayed were disinfected. Over a period of 13 months 272 people suffered this illness. T. J. Dyke, medical officer for the Local Board of Health for Merthyr Tydfil, urged the Board of Guardians to provide sufficient hospital accommodation for paupers to enable them to be isolated and thereby prevent the spread of the disease. It was the erection of a wooden hospital in Dowlais in 1870 by the Local Board of Health which made it possible to bring the epidemic to an end.

The cost-conscious Board of Guardians were not prepared to incur extra expense on this occasion:

'*Moved by Mr. Simons, Seconded by Mr. Gould*
   That the Board not having sufficient accommodation in the Fever ward for Fever pauper cases, application be made to the Merthyr Board of Health for the use of the Bryant's Field Hospital and the Dowlais Hospital.
Amendment Moved by Mr. Rees H. Rhys, Seconded by Mr. Jas. Lewis
   That the information before the board is not sufficient to make it expedient to adopt any extraordinary measures to meet the alleged outbreak of Fever

The Board divided

For Motion	For Amendment
The Chairman	*Mr. Jno. W. James*
Mr. W. L. Daniel	*Mr. Jno. Williams*
Mr. Thos. Williams	*Mr. Jno. Smith*
Mr. Wm. Gould	*Mr. David Watkins*
Mr. Wm. Simons	*Rev. G. C. J. Harris*
Rev. Jno. Griffith	*Mr. Jno. Perrott*
Mr. Geo. Martin	*Mr. Dd. Davis*
	Mr. Evan Lewis
	Mr. James Lewis
	Mr. Rees H. Rhys

Amendment carried'

(Minutes MTBG, 3 Dec. 1870).

The parsimony of the Board of Guardians and the appalling conditions under which some of the victims existed were described by the *Merthyr Express*:

'*Relapsing Fever/Typhus in Merthyr Tydfil*

Mr. Daniel said he wished to call the attention of the Guardians to the state of fever in Merthyr, and when they knew what it was, they would confess that things were in a very bad state indeed. At his request, Mr. Roberts, the relieving officer, had favoured him with the amount that he had given in relief and in kind

in the upper district of Merthyr since the 1st December, and it had appeared had given £28.8.3d to fever cases in that period. It would be very much wiser and more economical if the moment a person were taken in fever he should be removed into the wards of the infirmary and thereby save the enormous expense that occurred, not to the parish, but to the Union in the way of giving relief to those cases out of doors.'
(*ME* 15 Jan. 1870).

Far more serious was the smallpox epidemic of 1871. This crisis exposed the conflict between the Board of Guardians and the Local Board of Health. Starting in November 1871, smallpox had claimed 83 deaths by April 1872, and 1,342 cases were listed in the parish of Merthyr Tydfil alone (PRO MH12/16335, 3 May 1872). Both the Poor Law and Public Health bodies in Merthyr Tydfil would have enforced the Diseases Prevention Act of 1855, but were forbidden to do so by the Local Government Board which believed that the disease could be controlled by vaccination. This proved difficult because people refused to co-operate. Dr. T. J. Dyke wrote to Sir John Simon, medical officer of the Local Government Board, pointing out that for the past two months people in the area had been victims of the superstition that insufficient protection was given by vaccination. Such blind obstinacy meant that nothing could be gained by vaccination alone.

The *Merthyr Express* exposed the problems associated with the epidemic when reporting Dr. T. J. Dyke's report to the Merthyr Tydfil Local Board of Health:

'Medical Officer's Report - Startling Accounts of Smallpox.
. . . The pestilence of small-pox still continues to spread widely among the people. In the fortnight ending 27 April, 101 new cases were reported from the Dowlais and Penydarren Wards, and 189 from the Town, Cyfarthfa and Plymouth Wards, a total of 290 new cases.

The whole number of cases of sickness reported now amounts to 1342; this on the estimated population would be equivalent to the infection of one out of 39.

The deaths from smallpox in the fortnight numbered 43. The total of deaths is 167.

The proportion of deaths of persons who had not been vaccinated was two out of five, while of those who had been vaccinated only one out of 25 died.

You and the public generally, will ask, how is the disease thus so widely spread? The answers are these: by the idle curiosity which leads people to the bedsides of the sick; the useless assembling of people in infected houses, and at funerals; the use of palls and hearses to cover and convey the bodies of the dead; the gathering together from all quarters of many children at schools, and the incautious exposure of persons recovering from the disease in places of public assembly.'
(*ME* 4 May 1872).

The inefficiency and confusion caused by administrative disorder in the Poor Law and Public Health sectors accentuated local problems still further. There were sick paupers over whom the Local Board of Health had no power to act, even though the Board of Guardians did not assume its proper responsibility for them. So serious was the situation in the Union, that in Aberdare alone in 1872, there were 921 cases of smallpox with 152 fatalities, and a Local Government Board inspector from London was sent to examine the problem (PRO MH12, 6 July 1872).

> '*The Clerk mentioned that Mr G Harris, Government Small-pox Inspector, had called upon him and drawn his attention to a matter which he would recommend the Board carry into effect. It was respecting the removal by force of persons suffering from contagious diseases, at the expense of the nuisance authority. The power was already vested in the Board of Health in Merthyr and Aberdare of moving such persons to their hospitals if there were a deficiency of proper accommodation for them in their own homes, and it was also advisable that paupers similarly afflicted should be moved to the Workhouse Infirmary ...*
>
> *The Rector wished to know whether in the case of a person dying of small-pox who was too poor to pay for a hearse and who had no friends to carry the coffin, it would be competent for the relieving officer to supply what was necessary, because a case of this nature had come under his notice during the past week, when considerable difficulty was experienced in getting anyone to carry the coffin.*
>
> *The Clerk replied that under the circumstances it would of course be the duty of the relieving officer to provide a hearse if application were made to him.*'
> (ME 8 June 1872).

Dr. Harris, the medical inspector, considered that the Guardians were too ready to foist their responsibilities on to the Local Board of Health. He instanced a place in Cefn Coed-y-Cymmer, outside the jurisdiction of the health authority, where there were six or seven cases of smallpox at the time of his visit, none of whom had received any attention from the Board of Guardians. In respect of vaccination, better co-operation between vaccination officers and the medical officer of health would have enabled cases needing hospital treatment to be removed quickly. This report was received by the Guardians with bland indifference. However, it is noteworthy that the whole vaccination service was reviewed, with the result that in August 1873, the inspector of vaccination sent the Guardians a letter congratulating them on their administration of the Vaccination Acts.

The Board of Guardians was also reluctant to provide sufficient hospitals for sick paupers (PRO MH12/16335, 2 July 1872). South Wales, with its high percentage of single men in lodgings, was an area where epidemics were potentially disastrous, partly because of overcrowded dwellings. It was claimed that these young men were reluctant to go to hospital, but experience proved this to be untrue. It was an excuse to avoid the expense of building hospitals. At the time of the 1871 smallpox epidemic, the main provision made by the Board of Guardians was to place two wards at their workhouse infirmary at the disposal of pauper smallpox victims. This was an act of gross irresponsibility because the ward for sick children was located below. When 21 smallpox cases were brought into the infirmary, 13 inmates caught the disease, of whom 11 were children under the age of six. Profound ignorance of the nature of this disease produced appalling consequences.

The attitude of the Guardians is shown in these entries:

'*Ordered that the Medical Officers of Aberdare and Merthyr Parishes do give immediate notice to the Medical Officer of Health of those Parishes of all Pauper cases of Small Pox in which compulsory removal to a Hospital under the 26th Sec of the Sanitary Act 1866 is deemed necessary with a view to the Local Board taking steps to remove the Patients into the Workhouse, and that the Clerks of the Local Boards be also written to.*

St. Tydfil's hospital, formerly the workhouse, photographed in 1992, showing the rear of the women's wards and access to the basement.

Moved by Mr. Wm. Gould, Seconded by Rev. Jno. Griffith & Resolved
That the Merthyr Hearse be lent gratis to all persons requiring it for burial of contagious cases. Ordered that the Merthyr Hearse be painted and repaired and supplied with knobs.'
(Minutes MTBG, 1 June 1872).

'Read letter of Local Government Board of 5th July 1872 with extract of Report of Dr Harris Med. Inspector, and asking for this Board's observations thereon
Moved by Mr. Rees H. Rhys, Seconded by Mr. Thos. Williams & Resolved
*   That the Guardians do not consider Mr. Harris' report at all unsatisfactory, and that the attacks from Small Pox among the Inmates of the House do not exceed the average in the parish of Merthyr generally.'*
(Minutes MTBG, 6 July 1872).

In contrast, Merthyr Tydfil Local Board of Health provided two hospitals: one in the town area with 40 beds and one in Dowlais with 30 beds. Aberdare Local Board of Health set up a fever hospital made of galvanized iron and wood; it provided 40 beds, but was not opened until after the epidemic of 1871 had abated. By 1876, an arrangement was suggested whereby the Local Boards of Health for Merthyr Tydfil and Aberdare should be jointly responsible for the expense and management of these hospitals (PRO MH12/16337, 9 Dec. 1876). After a great deal of discussion, the Local Government Board reluctantly agreed to this expedient in 1877. In future, two fever hospitals were to be kept open constantly, instead of reopening when an epidemic had become established. This was a major step forward towards controlling infectious diseases which, allied with the provision of a pure water supply and a sewerage system, gradually overcame the problems associated with serious epidemics.

'Resolved unanimously
A.   That it is expedient that the Board of Health Hospitals now established at Aberdare and Merthyr be maintained at the joint equal expense and under the joint management of the Union on the one hand and of the respective Local Boards on the other, for the reception of cases of infectious disease.
B.   That the cost of the maintenance of each Hospital be borne in the first instance by the Board of Health, and that the Union refund one half of the cost at the end of every Halfyear
C.   That the infectious Hospitals at Merthyr be managed by a joint Committee to consist of 4 Guardians and 4 Members of the Merthyr Local Board, and that the infectious Hospital at Aberdare be managed by a joint Committee to consist of 4 Guardians and 4 Members of the Aberdare Local Board, and that both Committees may meet for general purposes as one Committee.
*   That copies of the foregoing resolutions be sent to the Clerks of the Aberdare and Merthyr Local Boards.'*
(Minutes MTBG, 22 July 1876).

To the category of sick paupers, could be added that of lunatics and also the aged who were ailing and becoming feeble-minded. Lunatics were a class of paupers who were treated as an exception to the prohibition of outdoor relief. When they were admitted to workhouses as inmates, however, no proper accommodation was provided for them. As late as 1909, the *Minority Report of the Royal Commission on the Poor Laws and Relief of Distress*, described the 'terrible sights' they had seen in workhouses: '*We have seen feeble-minded boys growing up in the workhouse year after year, untaught, untrained, alternately neglected and tormented by other inmates . . . We have seen idiots who are physically offensive or mischievous, or so noisy as to create a disturbance by day and by night with their howls, living in the ordinary wards . . . We have seen expectant mothers come in for their confinements, by day and night, working, eating and sleeping in close companionship with idiots and imbeciles of revolting habits and hideous appearance*'.

Some of the lunatics in this Union were sent to county asylums, but the difficulty of recovering part of the cost from their relatives prevented the whole-hearted adoption of this policy. Prior to the opening of the workhouse in 1853, paupers in this class were either placed in institutions or boarded out with friends and relations. Thus in 1844, six were in asylums at a cost of 8/- a week, and 18 were in receipt of outdoor relief at a cost of 3s. 8½d. a week. The institutions used for this purpose were at Bailbrook near Bath, Bridlington, Devizes and Briton Ferry.

The report of Dr. J. W. James, the surgeon, after visiting the Briton Ferry asylum concluded:

> '*To sum up: I may observe that Mr. Leach remarks that the cases sent by the Merthyr Tydfil Union are the worst set of cases he has to deal with and are not sent in the early stages. The condition of the patients is below the average, but the patients do not complain of want of food.*
>
> *Anne Treharne and Richard Watkins are the only two patients whom I might venture to say fit to be removed. I might however observe that one day is not sufficient to form an accurate judgment of the ordinary condition of these patients, because they vary exceedingly at different periods.*'

(Minutes MTBG, 2 Nov. 1849).

In 1859, an annual return showed that from Merthyr Tydfil Union, 29 lunatics were housed at Briton Ferry asylum and two at Abergavenny hospital (PRO MH12/16331, 20 Feb. 1859). A watchful eye was kept by the superintending inspector on irregular removals. When three paupers were taken from Briton Ferry asylum in 1858, allegedly for transference to Abergavenny hospital, two of them went into the workhouse and the other one was sent to relatives. The inspector informed the Guardians that it was illegal to do this (PRO MH12/16331, 9 Aug. 1858).

The proposal to establish a county lunatic asylum at Bridgend was supported by the Guardians, though when it finally materialised in 1865, they complained that its costs were too high (Minutes MTBG, 2 June 1869). By March 1872, there were 113 paupers from Merthyr Tydfil Union at Bridgend asylum and

A woman in Bedlam. Detail from a drawing by George Cruikshank, 1839.

five in Abergavenny asylum at a cost of 9/- per person per week. The average cost for an indoor pauper in the workhouse at this time was 3s. 4½d. per week (*Merthyr Tydfil Union Abstracts*, March 1872). It is therefore not surprising that the Guardians sent to the asylum only those too violent and too dangerous to be in the workhouse.

The Lunacy Commissioners, appointed under the terms of the Lunacy Act 1845, were obliged to visit all asylums, hospitals and workhouses where lunatics were kept. Two of them, one legal and one medical, visited hospitals and workhouses once a year, while private asylums were visited twice a year. In 1854, when they visited Merthyr Tydfil workhouse, they saw only three female pauper lunatics whom they described as tranquil and in good bodily health (PRO MH12/16329, 24 June 1854). In September 1857, the Commissioner expressed concern about two who were kept permanently in bed. He considered that, unless they could be given regular exercise, it would be wiser to send them to Briton Ferry asylum. In October 1861, the Commissioner recorded his approval that lunatics were taken regularly beyond the workhouse grounds for walks. Extra food was allotted to them in the form of three meat dinners a week and extra 'comforts' such as a table, a few chairs and some suitable periodicals (PRO MH12/16331, 10 Oct. 1861).

The case of Simon Vincent, a pauper lunatic at the workhouse, created a stir in 1867 (PRO MH12/16333, 15 Aug. 1867). He was removed on 2 July 1867 to Bridgend asylum where he died on 6 August. The Commissioners of Lunacy blamed the relieving officer for not having removed him earlier. The cause of death was given as *'general paralysis hastened by profuse subcutaneous suppuration of the right leg and left arm'*, which originated in wounds on the wrist and ankle caused by his being tied down before being taken to the asylum. The workhouse master admitted that Vincent had been put into a straight-jacket which he had torn to pieces, and that handcuffs had been put on his wrists. The relieving officer had been unable to remove him on 30 June as it was the payment day for outdoor paupers. When he took him on 2 July, Vincent had gone peacefully. This whole incident was viewed by the Poor Law Board with strong disapproval.

The treatment of lunatics in the workhouse came in for further criticism when the Commissioners for Lunacy visited it in 1868 (PRO MH12/16333, 22 June 1868). Out of five male and seven female lunatics, two women in the infirmary were in a disgusting condition. Not only were they dirty in person, but their rooms and bedding were also dirty and in disorder. One of the bedrooms contained ten beds instead of eight, and, in the opinion of the Commissioner, the chaff pillows should have been replaced with something softer. The bathroom was used for storing dirty linen and bedding, and was in a state of complete disorder. Five imbeciles of either sex, placed in the main body of the house with other paupers, were in a better condition.

By the next visit of the Lunacy Commissioners in 1871, improvements had been made (PRO MH12/16334, 27 July 1871). There were 12 pauper lunatics in the workhouse of whom four were women 'usefully employed'. They were all on a No 2 diet which entitled them to meat and beer every day. The medical officer in the workhouse objected to this but the Commissioner insisted that it should continue and that once a month, they should see any friends they might have.

The number of lunatics in the workhouse varied from 13 in September 1874 to 35 in October 1894. They were said to be harmless cases who were allowed to mix freely with ordinary inmates, but the visiting Lunacy Commissioner in 1874 gave a totally different impression (PRO MH12/16336, 28 Sep. 1874). He was critical of the dormitories which were improperly ventilated and he pointed out the lack of proper sanitary facilities. He was dismayed to find that the inmates diet had been reduced and disappointed to find that the Board of Guardians would allow them only chaff beds.

In 1894, the condition of the lunatics in the workhouse was summed up in the Lunacy Commissioner's Report (PRO MH12/16349, 3 Sep. 1894). They were still mixed indiscriminately with other inmates and some of the imbecile epileptics were even trusted with dangerous tools such as hatchets. The Commissioner expressed surprise that a serious accident had not already occurred. There was insufficient separation of the sexes and too little supervision. With so many imbeciles to be cared for, it was suggested that they should be placed in special wards with paid attendants. The ultimate solution lay in their removal from the workhouse altogether, but this was still a long way off.

THE AGED

In relation to the aged, the official policy of granting outdoor relief remained unchanged throughout the period under discussion. Neither the Report nor the Act of 1834 had suggested that outdoor relief should be abolished or even restricted to this class, as was emphasised by the Assistant Commissioner in his first address to the Board of Guardians at Merthyr Tydfil in November 1836 (*CMG* 12 Nov. 1836). At that time, there were 133 old men and 302 old women receiving poor relief. Some of them experienced acute distress when poor relief to non-resident paupers in South Wales was restricted on the orders of the Poor Law Commissioners (*CMG* 4 Feb. 1837). The effects were soon felt in the Merthyr Tydfil Union where paupers of advanced age had been receiving weekly relief from distant Unions.

Under the new system, they were told they had either to return to the parishes where they had a settlement or go without relief. Some old people had sons, daughters or other relatives in the area who were too poor to keep them; some were widows of workmen who had never seen the parishes in which their husbands had had a settlement. They had such a horror of going to strangers, or being offered the workhouse, that in many cases they went in fear of starvation rather than face an order of removal. Brecon Union refused to relieve any parishioners unless they were sent back to their respective parishes which affected one pauper who was 99 years of age, and several over 80, then living in Merthyr Tydfil Union.

'*Ordered the Clerk write to the Brecon Union in behalf of Thomas Powell aged 87 years, who states he was born in the parish of Llandefailog fach at Sarny, that his father's name was Howell Powell a labourer at that place, that he, the applicant worked in the parish of Llandefailog nearly 50 years as a weaver, and left many years since for Merthyr Tydfil, that he lived as a servant with the Penydarran Iron Co. for 27 years and never did any act to gain a settlement - request 2/6d a week for the applicant and state that this Board appeals with confidence to the humanity of the Brecon Board on behalf of the poor old man.*'
(Minutes MTBG, 16 March 1839).

'*Ordered that Thomas Powell be placed under an order of removal to his parish.*'
(Minutes MTBG, 4 May 1839).

In general, the Board of Guardians was fully prepared to provide for the aged by means of outdoor relief. The attempt of the Poor Law Board to insist that at least one third should be in kind (i.e. bread) was strongly resisted. The Guardians regarded it as an unjustifiable interference in their discretionary powers and claimed that they were '*better acquainted with the proper way of carrying out the details of the Act of Parliament than any body of Commissioners or*

Inspectors residing in London' (PRO MH12/16329, 6 Nov. 1852). They threatened to resign *en masse* if such an order were to be enforced. So strong was the general opposition to this measure that the Poor Law Board abandoned it. Thereafter, the aged and infirm received outdoor relief in cash payments and were merged into the whole body of paupers and little or no attention was paid to them until 1871.

It was in 1871 that a change of policy was introduced by the Local Government Board towards the aged, by advocating the workhouse test on the grounds that it would lead to the poor providing for their old age, for sickness and for widowhood. It is difficult to know how people on the poverty line could make that provision. Such a policy was ignored in Merthyr Tydfil Union which continued to grant outdoor relief, even increasing it during periods of severe weather. These grants were made in January 1881, December 1882, January 1887 and January 1891, at the rate of 6d or 1/- a week extra. Though Inspector Bircham of the Local Government Board disapproved of it, because he thought each case should be considered on its own merit, he was prepared to concede that there was hardly an instance where extra relief was not needed (PRO MH12/16348, 17 Jan. 1891). When Queen Victoria's Jubilee was celebrated in May 1887, the aged and sick were even granted an extra payment of one shilling. In general, they were not required to attend before the Board of Guardians after their first appearance; a rota committee was allowed to deal with them in the parish where they lived (Minutes MTBG, 14 Dec. 1889). For more than two decades, this Board of Guardians ran counter to official policy on the aged without being challenged.

VAGRANTS

It has already been noted that in this populous Union vagrants were an intractable problem. The policy recommended in the Poor Law Report of 1834, that they should be treated in the same way as able-bodied paupers, was a conspicuous failure. Workhouses simply afforded the habitual tramp a national system of well-ordered and suitably-situated lodging houses. This was realised by the Merthyr Board when they petitioned the Poor Law Board in 1869.

'... *the Board has received, and considered your Circular on the subject of Vagrancy.*
   We fully believe with you in the absolute necessity of discriminating, by careful investigation between real and simulated destitution, and we believe further that this can best be done by causing all Tramps to be relieved by the Police.'
(Minutes MTBG, 20 Feb. 1864).

The Poor Law Board had urged discrimination between deserving travellers and professional vagrants by issuing tickets to honest wayfarers and accommodation in the workhouse without task work. This produced a storm of opposition. The Guardians objected to wards for tramps in the workhouse and refused to have one because they considered it would be like setting up a hotel for 'illicit travellers'. They also opposed the issuing of tickets because they believed that 'under a system of passports, the greatest rogue would always have his papers in order'.

Instead, they followed a practice introduced in 1849 whereby the superintendent of police at Merthyr Tydfil and a sergeant of police at Aberdare carried out the work of relieving vagrants in return for a salary of £15 a year. These officers gave tickets of admission to lodging houses for 3d. a night. In cases of urgent necessity, an order was given for food from the workhouse and from a shop at Aberdare. In the former, the allocation was 8 ozs of bread; for the latter, 2d. to buy bread and cheese was allowed. Even so, vagrancy increased, reaching the figure of 3,442 for the half year ending March 1869 (*Merthyr Tydfil Union Abstracts*, March 1869). To deal with this formidable

'Found in the street.' Applying for admission to a 'refuge'. Drawn by Gustave Doré.

problem more effectively, the Guardians set up a committee to report on alternative solutions (Minutes MTBG, 18 Sep. 1869). It recommended that magistrates and police should be asked to detain all professional tramps and proceed against them under the Vagrancy Acts. The police should also prosecute wanderers and refuse relief except in cases of sickness or accidents.

However, by refusing relief to '*worthless wanderers*', they made them into '*masterful beggars*', while in periods of unemployment, those genuinely in need suffered terrible hardship or even death. Considering the alleged effectiveness of their treatment of vagrants (tramps), the Merthyr Tydfil Board of Guardians showed great concern about the problem, which was more deep-rooted and complex than the Tramp Committee realised. Certainly, the figures were alarmingly high during the 1860s.

> '*Upon referring to the Tramp Book it appears with few exceptions the Tramps relieved are in the prime of life, and that many of them are artisans in trades in which there is ample employment at the places from which the Tramps profess to have come - that others are sailors who appear to be wandering inland as vagrants, and others appear to be well persons wandering about and avoiding work.*
>
> *The Committee recommended that the Magistracy and the Police authorities be requested to direct the Police to apprehend all professed Tramps found in the district of this Board, and to proceed against them under the Vagrancy Acts.*'
> (Minutes MTBG, 16 Sep. 1869).

It is interesting to note that during the period of intermittent industrial strife between 1871 and 1875, when there was intense hardship, the number of vagrants given poor relief actually fell. This was partly because of the sterner measures employed by the Board of Guardians, partly because of the lack of work in the area for those genuinely searching for it, and partly because of a reduction in public charity offered to professional beggars. Vagrancy was a recurring problem despite harsh measures, so that by 1894 it was becoming increasingly clear that Poor Law principles could not be divorced from trade fluctuations and seasonal employment.

Conclusion

The problem of poverty in Merthyr Tydfil Union during a period of rapid industrialisation, enormous demographic changes and violent social upheavals, illustrates clearly the total inadequacy of a system of poor relief based on the concept that poverty was due to a moral fault in the individual. The Poor Law Amendment Act of 1834, for all its centralisation of authority and its bureaucracy, was bound to fail because of its incomplete diagnosis of the problems it tried to control. The New Poor Law caused enormous suffering before it was eventually replaced by a more humane approach. It has to be remembered, however, that it reflected social thinking in Victorian times and it is necessary to understand it, rather than to condemn it with hindsight.

In the 1830s, and until the end of the century, it was believed that every person should be able to fend for himself, and that self-help was to be encouraged. This derived from the philosophy of an industrial, entrepreneurial society. As society became more industrialised and urban, there came the gradual realisation that men could not be thought of as separate entities and masters of their own fates, because they were often at the mercy of forces far greater than themselves. Boards of Guardians such as those in Merthyr Tydfil Union quickly realised that it was impossible to refuse outdoor relief even to the able-bodied in industrial towns during severe trade depressions. In practical terms, they also came to realise that it was far more expensive to keep paupers in a workhouse than it was to give outdoor relief to tide them over. While the spirit of the Poor Law Report had to be modified in practice, yet the rigour it demanded remained. This was summed up by a statement made as late as 1905 by J. S. Davy, Assistant Secretary of the Local Government Board, '*That though a man in need through no fault of his own was entitled to sympathy, he must stand by his accidents; he must suffer for the general good of the body politic*'. What Davy failed to realise was that it was no longer sufficient to intimidate a pauper into not being a pauper. The question was at last being asked *why* people became paupers.

The history of poor relief in the Merthyr Tydfil Union provides a telling illustration of the shortcomings of such a system. The supposedly self-acting principles of 'less eligibility' and 'the workhouse test' produced very different results from those intended. Expenditure on the poor rose steadily from £5,202 9s.8d. for the year ending March 1838 to £21,373 6s.0d. for the year ending March 1853 (See Appendix 8). After the building of the workhouse in 1853, there was an initial fall in the number of people receiving relief, but disillusionment soon crept in. The workhouse was neither cheap to run nor well-adapted to deal with periods of unemployment. From 1857 onwards, total expenditure remained well above that before 1853, though the number of paupers was fewer. The marked increase in both numbers and expenditure in the late 60s, and early 70s, was due to the heavy burden of sickness and of unemployment which rose to a peak during the prolonged strike of 1875. These catastrophes exposed both the inhumanity and inadequacy of the system in face of economic and social change of vast proportions. Though both indoor and outdoor relief continued on a massive scale, and the workhouse failed to produce the expected decline in numbers, yet some progress was made in the technique of administering the Poor Law. However, the fact remained that pauperism was an intractable problem which could not be separated from trade fluctuations and social conditions. The growing realisation of this fundamental truth led to the modification of the New Poor Law.

Merthyr Tydfil Union Board of Guardians was the product of its time. The attitude of the Guardians towards poor relief was that laid down by the Central Authority, though when it was expedient to do so, the Guardians could take an unorthodox approach based on convenience and self-interest. The Board was dominated by ironmasters, coal-owners and property-owners whose interests as major ratepayers determined their decisions as Guardians. The inordinate delay in building a workhouse in Merthyr Tydfil was due not only to an unwillingness to spend ratepayers' money on an unpopular institution, but also to a fear that it might provoke insurrection among the masses of workers, in a volatile situation. The masters' over-riding need was to maintain a flexible and law-abiding labour-force.

The system of poor relief which the Guardians implemented may appear harsh to the twentieth-century reader but it was that laid down by the Poor Law Amendment Act of 1834. H. A. Bruce and G. T. Clark might on the one hand show paternalistic concern about the scandalous condition of orphan pauper children and sick paupers, while on the other they were quick to castigate able-bodied men who came out on strike. The policy of the 1834 Act determined the nature of poor relief provided. Even though the radical element in the Merthyr Tydfil Board of Guardians (the James family and their connections), challenged the autocracy of the ironmasters and some of the worst features of the system of poor relief, they themselves could do little to overthrow the former or to change the latter.

THE END OF THE POOR LAW

By the end of the nineteenth century, it was clear that reform of Local Government and the Poor Law was needed. The Local Government Act of 1888 created County Councils, and an Act of 1894 Urban and Rural District Councils. Boards of Guardians continued to function alongside them, often exercising overlapping powers. In 1905, a Royal Commission was appointed to examine the Poor Law. When it reported in 1909, the Commissioners recommended the abandonment of the concept of the deterrent Poor Law and the principle of less eligibility. The majority of the Commissioners wished to replace the Poor Law Authority with a Public Assistance Division of the Local

Government Board. The minority of the Commissioners, on the other hand, recommended the complete break-up of the existing Poor Law system and the transference of power to committees run by County and County Borough Councils which would deal with various categories of paupers.

The demise of the Poor Law was a long and complicated process, not completed until after the Second World War. The 'Five Freedoms' emphasised by the Beveridge Report in 1942, and the election of a Labour Government in 1945 pledged to implement these ideals in the post-war period, sounded the final death-knell for the Poor Law. By 1948, with the introduction of a state medical service and the passing of the National Assistance Act of that year, the break-up of the old system was complete. At last, problems of health, sickness, old age, destitution, unemployment and housing were viewed as a whole. The Welfare State had arrived.

Merthyr Tydfil Union, Area and Population

Parishes	Area in Acres	POPULATION						
		1831	1841	1851	1861	1871	1881	1891
Aberdare	16,858	3,961	6,471	14,998	33,247	37,704	35,514	40,906
Gelligaer	16,388	825	3,215	3,807	5,777	9,192	11,592	12,754
Merthyr	17,714	22,083	34,978	46,389	49,810	51,891	48,857	58,080
Penderyn	12,765	1,385	1,488	1,775	1,331	1,668	1,598	1,433
Rhigos	5,420	505	615	1,047	822	863	1,008	964
Vaynor	6,597	1,933	2,286	2,667	2,984	2,792	2,851	3,057
TOTAL	75,742	31,692	49,053	70,683	92,971	104,110	101,420	117,194

(*Merthyr Tydfil Union Abstract of Accounts*, October 1894).

'Mr. Bumble degraded in the eyes of the Paupers'.
In the background, women paupers work in the laundry.
Cruikshank's illustration in *Oliver Twist*, 1838.

APPENDIX 2

Poor Law Commission Office, Somerset House, London 1836

GENTLEMEN,

As many of you have been suddenly and unexpectedly called upon to perform the duties which have devolved upon you as Guardians for the administration of relief to the poor within the district comprehended by your Union, and as those duties are altogether new in their character, the COMMISSIONERS OF POOR LAWS FOR ENGLAND AND WALES submit to you the following explanations, in the hope that they may assist you in the execution of the duties of your most important office.

The chief, and perhaps the most important, officer of the Union is the Clerk to the Board of Guardians. The Commissioners, therefore, request your special attention to the statement of his duties, as set forth in the Rules and Regulations for the management of the Board, that you may be fully aware of the necessity of setting aside all local feelings and partialities in selecting the fittest obtainable person for the situation.

The appointments of the Relieving Officers will next, in due course, be brought under deliberation.

It will be their duty to conduct the preparatory changes of the existing system of out-door relief. It will be their business to investigate the existing claims and all new claims to relief, and to administer relief strictly according to the statute, and in conformity to the regulations of the Poor Law Commissioners . . .

(Extract from *The First Annual Report of The Poor Law Commissioners*. Quoted in Anstruther, 1984, p. 75).

APPENDIX 3

Accidents in Aberdare Collieries

'In this valley, within five years past, there have been killed not fewer than 100 persons from explosions of fire-damp. Unless one of these catastrophes includes a score or two of human beings, it passes away unnoticed by the public. Many fatal explosions are never reported in the public papers. Ventilation is still very imperfect in what are called the "fiery pits". Nowhere could I find in use Mr. Foudrinier's admirable apparatus for preventing the cage being drawn over the pulley, and for stopping the cage in its descent, should the rope break. I have pointed out the insufficiency and the danger of ventilation by furnaces at the bottom of an upcast shaft, and the necessity that exists for a capstan or horse-gin, to be resorted to as a motive power for increasing the flow of pure air, whenever an accident may disable such a machine as Mr. Struvé's from working.

In the year 1845 an explosion occurred in Aberdare valley, in which twenty-five lives were lost; and again at the close of last summer, a second tremendous explosion (this time in a colliery not far distant, called the Llety Shenkin Colliery), by which fifty-two human beings were killed. It is right that the public should know that within five weeks of the last mentioned frightful accident, two more explosions occurred in the same pit, by which two men were burned; this was kept as private as possible. I made some inquiries into the distress which Llety Shenkin's accident occasioned, and I found that there were remaining in the parish nineteen widows, of whom four were left each with five children, the respective ages of the oldest being 19, 12, 11, and 9; others were left with four—three widows with two—young children. There were four families left without either parent, the mothers having died before the accident. All these were left unprovided for, and I was informed that nothing whatever had been done by the proprietor, either towards assisting the widows or the children. It is only just that I should state what he actually did—he paid for a coffin, with handles, for each corpse. In the former accident alluded to, the proprietor of the colliery made the widows and children a weekly allowance; and he showed some sagacity in promising and giving each widow a small fortune of £15 on marriage—a stroke of policy which, I have been assured was eminently successful, for in due time he married off every one of them.' (Ginswick, 1983, p. 133).

APPENDIX 4

The Irish in Merthyr Tydfil

The Correspondent of *The Morning Chronicle* described what he saw of the Irish settlers in Merthyr Tydfil and Dowlais.

'My duty is to describe the labouring classes and the poor; and the Irish must not be overlooked. What, then, can I say of them? They are laborious, patient and light-hearted. On the other hand I have found them here filthy, sensual, crafty, quarrelsome and brutish in their habits. Their houses are unfurnished, foul and stinking; their children uncared for—barefoot, ragged, unwashed and uneducated. And this not from necessity but from natural habits. They are compelled to segregate in their dwellings, for the Welsh will not reside among them. They inhabit the lowest and worst quarters of the town'.

He referred to the Irish colony in Penydarren where conditions were primitive. In one of the houses visited, he saw in a closet, an old woman who was bed-ridden and was supported by the parish: 'she lay on a mass of woollen rags, spread on the floor, and she completely filled the closet. If it were not for the open door she must have died of suffocation. Her allowance was 2s a week, out of which she paid 6d for lodging; upon the remaining 1s 6d she subsisted and paid for attendance'.

The Correspondent accompanied Edward Davies, the Surgeon to the Dowlais Ironworks. He visited a patient in Pont-y-storehouse (China) who lived in what was originally a one-roomed house. 'One of the women ran out and soon returned with a candle, which she lit, and carried before us up a ladder, into the loft above . . . The room was formed simply of the slope of the roof; there was no window, but a tile had been displaced to admit a little air and light. The cobwebs hung in black films from the roof. On the right and left hand of the entrance were two beds . . . Stooping down with the candle over the bed on the right, the woman pointed to the man—who was in a raging fever. When the doctor had examined him the woman threw up the clothes at the foot of the bed, and showed us a poor child, emaciated from dysentry and from fever, and shivering on its sudden exposure to the air'. In all, 11 people lived in this one-roomed house; they slept four in each bed in the roof-space and three downstairs where there were no sleeping facilities. 'The stench of this house was unendurable, and we were glad to get away from it'.

During the cholera epidemic of 1849, many of the Irish fled, leaving their relatives to the care of the men-nurses and others engaged by the authorities 'There were instances where the inmates of an Irish house, on a death occuring, fled, carrying with them the key to the front door; and it was necessary, in order to save breaking in the door, to get out the corpse for interment through the front window'.

(Ginswick, 1983, pp. 64-67).

APPENDIX 5

Expenditure on Poor Relief in Merthyr Tydfil Union, 1843-1849

Year ended 29th September				
	1843	£8599	18	4
	1844	8871	1	2
	1845	8432	7	1
	1846	7081	3	5
	1847	8727	5	4
	1848	12487	11	0
	1849	10034	2	5
Total (7 years)		£63733	8	9

Poor rates paid by the Merthyr Ironmasters
for the Quarter ending 25th December 1849.

Dowlais Iron Company	£697	11	0
Pen-y-darran British Iron Co	345	10	0
Cyfarthfa	559	16	0
Plymouth Works	381	11	6
Total of the Quarter	£1984	8	6

(Ginswick, 1983, p. 86).

By extrapolation the Ironmasters' contribution for the whole of 1849 would be about £7.937 14s 0d. Comparison with the actual expenditure on poor relief, viz £10,034 2s 5d, shows how large a proportion the Ironmasters contributed.

APPENDIX 6

Workhouse Regulations

Orders and Regulations to be observed in the Workhouse of the . . . Union.

I. PAUPERS are to be admitted into the workhouse in any one of the following modes, and in no other; viz.—

By an order of the board of guardians, signified in writing by their clerk.

By a provisional order in writing, signed by an overseer, churchwarden or relieving officer.

By the master of the workhouse, without any such order, in case of any sudden or urgent necessity.

IV. As soon as a pauper is admitted, he or she shall be placed in the probationary ward, and shall there remain until examined by the medical officer of the workhouse.

VII. Before removal from the probationary ward, the pauper shall be thoroughly cleansed, and shall be clothed in the workhouse dress; and the clothes which he or she wore upon admission shall be purified and deposited in a place to be appropriated for that purpose, to be restored to the pauper on leaving the workhouse, or else to be used by the pauper as the Board of Guardians shall direct . . .

Discipline and Diet

XIII. All the paupers in the workhouse, except the sick, the aged and infirm, and the young children, shall rise, be set to work, leave off work, and go to bed, at the times mentioned in the accompanying table 'A', and shall be allowed such intervals for their meals as therein are stated; and these several times shall be notified by ringing a bell, and during the time of meals, silence, order and decorum shall be maintained.

XIV. Half an hour after the bell shall have been rung for rising, the names shall be called over in the several wards provided for the second, third, fifth and sixth classes, when every pauper belonging to the ward must be present, to answer to his or her name, and to be inspected by the master or matron.

XVIII. The boys and girls who are inmates of the workhouse shall, for three of the working hours at least every day, be respectively instructed in reading, writing, and in the principles of the Christian religion; and such other instructions shall be imparted to them as are calculated to train them to habits of usefulness, industry and virtue.

XIX. The diet of the paupers shall be so regulated as in no case to exceed, in quantity and quality of food, the ordinary diet of the able-bodied labourers living within the same district . . .

XXII. Any pauper may quit the workhouse, upon giving the master three hours' previous notice of his wish to do so; but no able-bodied pauper having a family shall so quit the house without taking the whole of such family with him or her, unless the board of guardians shall otherwise direct; nor shall any pauper, after so quitting the house, be again received into the house, unless in one of the modes prescribed in Rule I. for the admission of paupers.

XXVI. Any pauper, who shall neglect to observe such of the foregoing rules as are applicable to him or her;

Or who shall make any noise when silence is ordered;

Or use obscene or profane language;

Or by word or deed insult or revile any other pauper in the workhouse;

Or who shall not duly cleanse his or her person;

Or neglect or refuse to work;

Or pretend sickness;

Or disobey any of the legal orders of the master or matron, or other superintendent;

shall be deemed disorderly, and shall be placed in apartments provided for such offenders, or shall otherwise be distinguished in dress, and placed upon such diet as the board of guardians shall prescribe.

XXVII. Any pauper who shall, within seven days, repeat one of the offences specified in Rule XXVI;

Or who shall by word or deed insult or revile the master or matron, or any officer of the Union;

Or who shall be guilty of any act of drunkenness or indecency;

shall be deemed to be refractory, and shall be punished by such confinement and alteration of diet as the board of guardians shall direct, by any regulation for that purpose; but no pauper shall be confined under this rule for any misbehaviour or offence, for a longer period than 24 hours, or for such further space of time as may be necessary, in order to have such pauper carried before a justice of the peace, to be dealt with according to law.

(Anstruther, 1984, pp. 93-95).

Arrival at the Workhouse. Drawing by John Leech
in *Jessie Phillips, A Tale of the Present Day*, 1844.

APPENDIX 7

Duties of Workhouse Master and Matron

The following shall be the duties of the master of the workhouse:-

1. To admit paupers into the workhouse, and to cause them to be examined by the medical officer, and to cleanse, clothe, and place them in the proper wards, according to the regulations herein established.

2. To enforce industry, order, punctuality, and cleanliness, and the observance of the several rules herein contained, by the paupers in the workhouse, and by the several officers, servants and other persons therein employed.

3. To read prayers to the paupers before breakfast and after supper every day, or cause them to be read, at which all the inmates must attend; but if any of the paupers shall profess religious principles indisposing them to unite in such service, they are to be permitted to sit apart, and not be compelled to join in the same.

4. To inspect and call over the names of all the paupers immediately after morning prayers every day, and see that each individual is clean, and in a proper state.

5. To provide for and enforce the employment of the able-bodied adult paupers during the whole of the hours of labour; to train the youth in such employment as will best fit them for service; to keep the partially disabled paupers occupied to the extent of their ability; and to leave none who are capable of employment idle at any time.

6. To visit the sleeping wards of the first, second, and third classes at 11 o'clock every day, to see that they have been all duly cleaned and properly ventilated.

7. To see that the meals of the paupers are properly dressed and served, and to superintend the distribution thereof.

8. To say or cause to be said grace before and after meals.

9. To see that the dining halls, tables, and seats, are cleaned after each meal.

10. To visit all the wards of the male paupers at nine o'clock every night, and see that all the male paupers are in bed, and that all fires and lights are extinguished.

11. To receive from the gatekeeper the keys of the workhouse at nine o'clock every night, and to deliver them to him again at six o'clock every morning.

The following shall be the duties of the matron of the workhouse:-

1. To see that the in-door work of the establishment is, as far as possible, performed by the female paupers maintained therein.

2. To provide for and enforce the employment of the able-bodied female paupers during the whole of the hours of labour; and to keep the partially disabled paupers occupied to the extent of their ability.

3. To visit all the wards of the females and children every night, and to ascertain that all the paupers in such wards are in bed, and the fires and lights duly extinguished.

4. To pay particular attention to the moral conduct and orderly behaviour of the female paupers and children; to see that they are clean and decent in their dress and persons, and to train them up in such employments as will best fit them for service.

5. To superintend and give the necessary directions for making and mending the clothing supplied to the female paupers and pauper children; and also the linen supplied to the male paupers of the Union; and to take care that all such clothing or linen be marked with the name of the Union.

6. To see that every pauper in the workhouse has clean linen and stockings once a week, and that all the beds be supplied with clean sheets once a month.

7. To take charge of the linen and stockings for the use of the paupers, and any other linen in use in the house, and to superintend and give the necessary directions concerning the washing, drying, and getting up the same, and not to permit any to be dried in the sleeping wards, or in the sick or lunatic wards.

8. To take care, with the assistance of the nurses, of the sick paupers and young children in the workhouse; to see that they are clean in their persons, and to provide such diet for the sick paupers and the young children as the medical officer shall direct, and to furnish them with such changes of clothes and linen as may be necessary.

9. To assist the master in the general management and superintendence of the workhouse, and especially in

Enforcing the observance of good order, cleanliness, punctuality, industry, and decency of demeanour among the paupers.

The cleansing and clothing of female paupers on their admission.

The cleansing and ventilating of the sleeping wards and the dining halls, and all parts of the premises.

The placing in store and taking charge of the provisions, clothing and linen belonging to the Union.

10. And generally to observe and fulfil all lawful orders and directions of the board of guardians, and the rules, orders and regulations issued by the Poor Law Commissioners . . .

(Anstruther, 1984, pp. 85-89).

APPENDIX 8

Expenditure on Pauperism and
Number of Paupers in Merthyr Tydfil Union

Year	Population	Expenditure	No. of Paupers Relieved	
			Indoor	Outdoor
1851	70,683	£21,598 : 19 : 3	—	15,320
1852		£21,373 : 6 : 0	—	14,600
1853		£21,028 : 16 : 10	419	8,797
1854		£20,265 : 16 : 0	774	7,770
1855		£18,507 : 18 : 5	823	7,948
1856		£22,663 : 19 : 4	815	9,823
1857		£24,128 : 12 : 8	872	10,895
1858		£24,876 : 8 : 4	932	11,678
1859		£25,610 : 3 : 8	991	10,837
1860		£25,260 : 19 : 5	1,179	11,470
1861	92,971	£29,640 : 13 : 0	1,557	13,752
1862		£27,984 : 2 : 0	1,494	14,796
1863		£29,585 : 13 : 9	1,394	13,640
1864		£29,329 : 13 : 6	1,233	13,149
1865		£28,919 : 7 : 0	1,338	13,125
1866		£33,311 : 10 : 4	1,048	14,455
1867		£33,441 : 8 : 6	1,293	17,158
1868		£36,166 : 12 : 7	1,767	18,451
1869		FIGURES ARE MISSING		
1870		£36,114 : 13 : 3	1,189	11,750
1871	104,110	£24,2410 : 14 : 3	1,277	10,305
1872		£33,896 : 12 : 9	1,048	4,530†
1873		FIGURES ARE MISSING		
1874		£16,752 : 10 : 2†	680†	5,410†
1875		£26,408 : 3 : 8†	683†	5,050†
1876		£33,075 : 13 : 0	1,160	6,838
1877		£30,817 : 18 : 2	1,265	8,307
1878		£32,429 : 5 : 9	1,145	9,054
1879		£29,759 : 5 : 10	1,127	9,177
1880		£29,038 : 15 : 10	1,027	8,519
1881	101,420	£33,274 : 1 : 8	971	9,010
1882		£26,016 : 18 : 11	967	7,879
1883		£26,325 : 11 : 5	898	7,089
1884		£26,844 : 0 : 5	1,039	6,383
1885		£27,595 : 19 : 6	969	6,478
1886		£25,567 : 14 : 3	1,153	7,160
1887		£29,886 : 5 : 5	961	7,267
1888		£25,126 : 13 : 2	1,017	7,297
1889		£24,747 : 9 : 1	1,041	7,296
1890		£19,649 : 2 : 7	1,163	7,980
1891	117,194	£28,756 : 9 : 4	1,474	6,920
1892		£28,602 : 16 : 9	1,590	7,122
1893		£31,284 : 12 : 3	1,875	9,048

(*Merthyr Tydfil Union Abstract of Accounts*, September 1850–October 1894).
† These figures are for the half-year only. The others are missing.

APPENDIX 9

Wages at Dowlais, 1850

'The various rates of wages paid to the men, as furnished to me by Mr. Howard, the intelligent and experienced cashier and superintendent of the books at Dowlais, to whose kind attention I am much indebted, are as follows:

Colliers' wages, 14s. a week
Miners' wages, 13s. a week
Founders' wages, 25s. a week
Furnace-fillers' wages, 24s. a week
Puddlers' wages, 17s. a week (this appears an average of
the puddler and his "second hand" who earns less)
Rollers' wages, 25s. a week
Ballers' wages, 18s. a week
Roughers' wages, 21s. a week
Labourers' wages, 10s. a week
Piling-girls' and mine-charing girls' wages, 5s. a week'

(Ginswick, 1983, p. 36).

APPENDIX 10

The Cost of Living, 1850

'Let us take the case of a "second hand" puddler, with a wife and four children under the statutable age for work; and consider the circumstances of his wages and his expenditure. He earns 15s a week, which may be regarded as the medium price of labour in and around Merthyr at the present time. Out of this he pays:

Rent (8s a month) weekly	2s.	0d.
Coal (6s 6d a month) weekly	1	$7\frac{1}{2}$
Doctor and Sick-fund	0	4
Clay for repairing furnace	0	4
Total	4s.	$3\frac{1}{2}$d.

This sum deducted from his weekly wages leaves just 10s $8\frac{1}{2}$d to feed and clothe six persons; his fiery and exhausting labour requiring that he should himself use animal food. One wonders how it can be done; yet, with the arts of thrift and good management, it is done by hundreds. The condition of labourers who earn only 10s a week is, of course, proportionately straitened and worse. This analysis of the cost and means of living amply corroborates the statements made to me, of the scanty and hard diet of these classes.'
(Ginswick, 1983, p. 55).

APPENDIX 11

Housing and Rents, 1850

'Houses for the best class of workmen ... are 10s to 13s a month. (Two rooms downstairs and two upstairs). There is no strip of garden, no backdoor or outlet ... no drain to carry away house refuse, nor any pump or pipe for the supply of water. The street in front is ... the receptacle of every kind of abomination conceivable.

The second class have but two rooms, the one above stairs and one below; for these the rents vary from 6s to 8s a month. There are third-class houses having only one room, for which the rent is about 4s a month'.
(Ginswick, 1983, p. 52).

APPENDIX 12

The Price of Food, 1850

'Beef or mutton (good) $4\frac{1}{2}$d. to $6\frac{1}{2}$d. per pound.
Pork, $4\frac{1}{2}$d. to 6d. per lb.
Fowls, per couple, 2s. to 3s. 6d.
Bacon (Welsh, home cured) 9d. to 10d. per lb.
Bacon (American), 6d. per lb.
Cheese (Gloucestershire and Caerphilly) 3d. to 7d. per lb.
Butter (salt) 7d., 8d., and $8\frac{1}{2}$d. per lb.
Butter (fresh) 10d. to 1s. per lb.
Flour (best quality) 3s. 4d. per 28 lbs.
Flour (seconds) 3s. to 3s. 2d. per 28 lbs.
Oatmeal (chiefly used by the Irish) 3s. 6d. per 28 lbs.
Indian meal (not much used) 2s. 6d. per 28 lbs.
Potatoes, $\frac{3}{4}$d. per lb. or 8 lbs. for 6d.
Candles (prodigious quantities are consumed in the mines and houses) 5d. to $5\frac{1}{2}$d. per lb.
Sugar (also largely used) 4d., 5d. and 6d. per lb.
Coffee, 10d. to 1s. 6d. per lb.
Tea, 3s. 8d. to 4s. 6d. per lb.
Soap (yellow) 5d. per lb. '
(Ginswick, 1983, pp. 51, 52).

Merthyr Tydfil Workhouse Buildings

Merthyr Tydfil Workhouse was opened in September 1853 at a cost of £6,880, excluding the cost of the land, and was intended to accommodate 500 paupers. The plans were provided by Messrs. Aickin and Capes of Islington, London. Some adaptations were necessary to effect economies, but on the whole the workhouse followed a conventional plan whereby the boundary walls formed a square, at the centre of which were two-storey buildings arranged in a cruciform pattern. In front, there was an additional range of buildings housing the chapel or boardroom, the porter's lodge and a reception area where new arrivals could be classified and given workhouse clothing, Here, in the receiving ward and washrooms, new entrants were stripped and bathed. The buildings situated against the outside walls provided facilities for task work, laundry work and for a mortuary which adjoined the graveyard. In Merthyr Tydfil, the provision of a separate schoolroom for girls within the front range was meant to ensure their segregation from other inmates and to relieve the over-crowding in the main schoolroom, in the cruciform building, where children between the ages of 2 and 15 were taught.

The central block also contained separate day rooms for men and women. On the first floor were situated dormitories, with the master's and matron's rooms separating the two sexes. On the top floor were more bedrooms, those of the boys and girls being separated by the 'lying-in' (maternity) ward and the nursery. Within the central block there was a dining room; this could also be used as a chapel. The workhouse kitchens, bakery and stores were located in the basement cellars which ran under the entire building. Each class of indoor paupers made use of separate exercise yards around the central block. Those who were sick were accommodated in outside wards within a building called the infirmary, *'in a high and healthy position'*. Separate provision was made whenever possible for cases of infectious diseases and for lunatics. Even the attics of the central block were used in emergencies to house children with infectious diseases.

The prison-like appearance of some of these buildings was intentional so as to strike terror into the hearts of the inmates. Though some parts have been modified to meet later requirements, and other parts have been demolished, enough remains to show the original character of the workhouse.

[The original set of building plans does not appear to have survived. The disposition of buildings can be seen, however, on the large-scale Ordnance Survey map].

Biographical Notes

The following biographical notes are included on some important people mentioned in the text. If they feature in the Dictionary of Welsh Biography, reference is made to that source.

BRUCE, Henry Austin (1815-1895), subsequently first Baron Aberdare. He was the second son of John Bruce Pryce, was called to the Bar from Lincoln's Inn and in 1847 became stipendiary magistrate for Merthyr Tydfil and Aberdare. In 1855, after the death of Sir Josiah John Guest, he became a trustee of Dowlais Ironworks. From 1852 to 1868, he represented Merthyr Tydfil in the House of Commons, and after his defeat, represented Renfrewshire from 1869 to 1873. He was appointed Home Secretary in 1873 and was transferred to the position of Lord President of the Council. In that same year, he was elevated to the peerage. He worked tirelessly in the cause of education and played a major part in achieving the Welsh Intermediate Education Act of 1889. He became first Chancellor of the University of Wales . (See DWB).

CLARK, George Thomas (1809-1898), engineer and antiquarian. Son of George Clark, he was educated at Charterhouse and qualified as an engineer. He worked under Brunel on the Great Western Railway. In 1852, he became a trustee of the Dowlais Ironworks and thenceforward until his death in 1898, he effectively controlled them. He played a leading part in local affairs, becoming Chairman of the Board of Guardians of Merthyr Tydfil Poor Law Union and Chairman of Merthyr Tydfil Local Board of Health. (See DWB).

CAMPBELL, James Colquhoun (1813-1895), became Rector of Merthyr Tydfil in 1844. He was the son of John Campbell of Stonefield, Argyll, and was educated at Trinity College, Cambridge. He was ordained as a priest at Llandaff in 1839 and subsequently became Vicar of Roath under Bute patronage. He married a daughter of John Bruce Pryce and was therefore a brother-in-law to Henry Austin Bruce. He owed his appointment at Merthyr Tydfil to Bute patronage. On his arrival, he set about learning the Welsh language and took a keen interest in the state of his parish which was undergoing dramatic social and economic changes.

In 1847, a new church (St. David's) and a National School were opened in Merthyr Tydfil. At this time, J. C. Campbell showed profound concern for the orphan pauper children who were boarded out in the 'cellars' of Pontystorehouse ('China'), where they lived in atrocious conditions. It was Campbell, in conjunction with H. A. Bruce (Stipendiary Magistrate of Merthyr Tydfil and ex-officio member of the Board of Guardians), who took the lead in exposing the scandalous condition of these children. During the cholera epidemic of 1849, it was Campbell who ministered fearlessly to the needs of the sick.

Controversy surrounds his rapid rise in the church to Honorary Canon of Llandaff Cathedral, Archdeacon of Llandaff (1858) and Bishop of Bangor

(1859-1890). Whatever enmity may have been felt against him because of his Scottish origins and Bute connection, the fact remains that when he left Merthyr Tydfil in 1859, tribute was paid to his 'exemplary piety, forbearance and unwearied zeal as a minister of the Gospel and as a pastor of the Church' and large numbers of his parishioners contributed to the presentation of plate on his departure. His elevation was marked by the award of the degree of Doctor of Divinity at Cambridge University. He resigned his see in 1890 and died in 1895 at the age of 82.

CRAWSHAY, William II (1788-1867), was manager of the Cyfarthfa and Hirwaun Ironworks and bought others in Treforest and the Forest of Dean. Known as 'the Iron King', he built Cyfarthfa Castle and also had a mansion at Caversham Park, Oxfordshire, where he died. Under the terms of his Will, the Cyfarthfa Works were left to his youngest son, Robert Thompson Crawshay, whose wife was Rose Mary Crawshay. (See DWB).

DAVIS, David (1797-1866), entered the coal trade in 1842 when he opened a small level at Cefn-Rhigos. In 1843, he took out a lease of the steam-coal seams at Blaengwawr in Aberdare and, in 1851, he sank a new pit at Abercwmboi. He was also attracted to the Rhondda Valley where he struck a good seam of coal in Ferndale. By 1865 he had become involved in opening up a new dock at Penarth for the export of coal. (See DWB).

FOTHERGILL, Richard (1822-1903), was an ironmaster, coal-owner and politician. He was the eldest son of Richard Fothergill II and became proprietor of Abernant Ironworks, Aberdare. In 1862, he acquired the Plymouth Ironworks and later the Penydarren Works passed into his hands, giving him great power and prestige. When Merthyr Tydfil and Aberdare qualified for two Members of Parliament in 1868, Richard Fothergill and Henry Richard were elected, defeating H. A. Bruce. (See DWB).

GRIFFITH, the Reverend John (1818-1885), was Vicar of Aberdare (1846-1859) and Rector of Merthyr Tydfil thereafter until his death. A controversial figure, he was criticised by the nonconformists for his defence of the 1846 Report on Education in Wales. He was also involved in attacks on the Anglican Church in respect of its indifference to the needs of Welsh-speaking communicants and its emphasis on ritualism. He was a staunch supporter of the movement for Disestablishment. Active in public life and possessing a strong social conscience, he became a member of Merthyr Tydfil Union Board of Guardians. (See DWB).

GUEST, Sir Josiah John (1785-1852) was an ironmaster, colliery-owner and Member of Parliament. Born at Dowlais, the son of Thomas Guest, ironmaster, he was educated at Bridgnorth and Monmouth Grammar Schools and was trained in the knowledge and techniques of iron-making. He showed great enterprise and by 1840 had raised the Dowlais Works to the position of the largest in the world. By 1851, he was the sole proprietor.

Guest was Member of Parliament for Honiton from 1825-1831, and when the parliamentary borough of Merthyr Tydfil was created in 1832, he was elected unopposed as its first Member of Parliament, a position he retained until his death. In July 1838, at the time of the coronation of Queen Victoria, Guest was made a baronet. He was heavily involved in local affairs and was a member of Merthyr Tydfil Board of Guardians and Merthyr Tydfil Local Board of Health. He promoted the Taff Vale Railway and became its first chairman. He established schools at Dowlais and extended his patronage to other cultural causes in the community.

Towards the end of his life, he lived at Canford Manor, Dorset, but he returned to Dowlais before he died on 26 November 1852 and was buried there. (See DWB).

GUEST, Lady Charlotte Elizabeth (1828-1895), was the daughter of Albemarle Bertie, ninth Earl of Lindsey and was married (1) to Josiah John Guest in 1833, (2) to Charles Schreiber in 1855. She proved to be a remarkable woman who translated 'The Mabinogion' into English with the aid of scholars. She took a keen interest in the education and welfare of the Dowlais Iron Company employees and their families. She was a great collector of china, fans and playing-cards, her china collection later being presented to the Victoria and Albert Museum. She died on 15 January 1895 at Canford Manor. (See DWB).

HILL, Anthony (1784-1862), son of Richard Hill I, he became manager of the Plymouth Ironworks, Merthyr Tydfil, and in 1842 was sole managing director of these works. He was regarded as the most scientific ironmaster in the area, being concerned with the search for better methods of iron manufacture. Plymouth Works bar-iron was renowned for its quality. He was an enlightened employer who showed concern for the social welfare of his workers. (See DWB).

JAMES, Christopher (1782-1861), moved from Whitchurch, Cardiff to Merthyr Tydfil where he built up a prosperous business in drapery, groceries and wine and his varied business interests at Merthyr Tydfil and Treforest brought him wealth. He became the spokesman for the carriers on the Glamorganshire Canal. His elder brother, William James (1781-1851), was a property-owner in Merthyr, and his younger brother, Job James (1788-1863), a surgeon (later employed as such by the Merthyr Tydfil Board of Guardians), was an admirer of the radical writer, William Cobbett.

From 1828 onwards, the James family and their connections became influential in the Merthyr Vestries, demanding reform. Unitarianism and political radicalism were to become distinctive features of their cause. Christopher James's eldest son, David William James (1805-1872) played an active part in Merthyr politics. When the first Board of Guardians was elected in 1836 he became its Vice-Chairman, and his influence was felt for the next thirty years. A cousin, Job James's son Dr. J. W. James, played a major part in the deliberations of the Board of Guardians during the crisis of the 1875 strike, when he and the former Chartist, William Gould, were virtually the only challengers of the ironmasters. William James's son, solicitor Charles Herbert James (1817-1890), represented Merthyr as a Liberal Member of Parliament between 1880 and 1888. (See DWB).

The important contribution of the 'James dynasty' to Merthyr politics merits further research. The main source of the above information is contained in *The Merthyr Rising*, by Professor Gwyn A. Williams (1978) and in *Communities*, by Professor Ieuan Gwynedd Jones (1987), supplemented by James family papers in the Glamorgan Record Office.

LEWIS, William Thomas (1837-1914), was a mining engineer who became mineral agent to the Marquess of Bute at the age of 27. In the same year, he married Anne, daughter of William Rees who owned Llety-Shenkin colliery in Aberdare. It was her grandfather, Robert Thomas, who had opened a colliery at Waun Wyllt, Abercanaid, Merthyr Tydfil, and started the sale of household coal, a trade which was developed after his death by his wife, Lucy, and his son, William.

William Thomas Lewis embarked upon interests of his own in the Rhondda and Rhymney valleys where he sank pits. He became a powerful influence in the coal trade and was a prime mover in developing the South Wales and Monmouthshire Coalowners' Association in 1872, in response to the growing trade unionism and strikes which occurred. He lived at Mardy House, Aberdare, and became first Baron Merthyr of Senghenydd. (See DWB).

MENELAUS, William (1818-1882), was born in Edinburgh and joined the Dowlais Ironworks as chief manager under Sir Josiah John Guest. After the latter's death in 1852, he became General Manager and ran the works efficiently until his own death in 1882.

NIXON, John (1815-1899), was a coal-owner and mining engineer. He sank the Werfa colliery in Aberdare, the Navigation colliery in Mountain Ash and bought Deep Duffryn colliery from David Williams. He opened up the steam-coal trade with France, thereby leading to great expansion in the coal industry. He introduced the 'long wall' system of mining and the 'double shift' into South Wales. He is credited with making improvements in the ventilation of mines.

POWELL, Thomas (1779-1863), began as a timber merchant in Newport but afterwards extended his activities to the coal trade. In 1840, he entered the steam-coal industry in the Aberdare valley where he sank a pit at Tir Founder in Cwmbach. He struck the four-feet seam and followed this by sinking the Plough, Lower Duffryn, Middle Duffryn and Upper and Lower Cefnpennar pits. His contact with Nixon enabled him to enter the French market and he was able to take advantage of the preference of the Admiralty for South Wales smokeless steam coal. He enjoyed outstanding success in the Aberdare valley and became one of the largest coal exporters in the world. After Powell's death, the Powell Duffryn Steam Coal Co. was formed in 1864 by Sir George Elliot. (See DWB).

PRICE, Thomas (1820-1888), was born near Brecon and served an apprenticeship as a painter, glazier and plumber. After a period in London, he entered Pontypool Baptist College in 1842, after which he became minister of Carmel Welsh Baptist Chapel (Capel Pen-Pound), Monk Street, Aberdare, in 1845, where he remained until his death. Well known as a preacher, lecturer and supporter of Friendly Societies (notably the Oddfellows and the Ivorites), he gained wide recognition by his participation in controversial issues. His attacks on the Reverend John Griffith, Vicar of Aberdare, in respect of his contribution to the 1846 Report on Welsh Education were renowned. At the time of the 1868 election in the constituency, Price was active and influential, though his standpoint on certain issues was questionable. He was given an honorary degree (Ph.D.) by the University of Leipzig and was a man of considerable local standing. He became a member of Merthyr Tydfil Union Board of Guardians and of Aberdare Local Board of Health. (See DWB).

RHYS, Rees Hopkin (1819-1899), was born and died at Plas Newydd, Llwydcoed, Aberdare. He became a mineral agent and was knowledgeable about the resources of Glamorgan and Monmouthshire. Unfortunately, in 1847, at the age of 28, he lost his sight in an explosion while conducting an experiment with gun-cotton at the Dowlais Works.

Despite his blindness, he played a unique part in public life in the area in which he lived. He was an influential member of Merthyr Tydfil Board of Guardians for 53 years, and played a leading part in setting up the Industrial School for pauper children at Aberdare. He was chairman of the Industrial School Committee from 1877 to 1887. In 1881, the Guardians, in recognition of his services, presented him with a bust of himself.

In 1854, he was elected a member of Aberdare Local Board of Health in which capacity he played an important part in providing a water supply, sewerage system and other public amenities in the area.

He was a magistrate, tax commissioner, a member of the Aberdare School Board and a governor of the University College of South Wales and Monmouthshire. He became a member of the Glamorgan County Council and was elected the first chairman of Aberdare Urban District Council at its first meeting on 4 January 1895.

Though he was a Unitarian, a memorial tablet to him was placed in St. John's Parish Church, Aberdare, which summed up his contribution as follows: 'By his great ability, foresight and strength of character, he proved himself as one of the ablest public servants of the nineteenth century'.

RICHARD, Henry (1812-1888), 'The Welsh Apostle of Peace', was born at Tregaron and trained for the ministry at Highbury College, London. In 1835, he was ordained at Marlborough Congregational Chapel, Old Kent Road, London. Early in his career, he became interested in the question of international peace and was appointed as secretary of the Peace Society. Passionately concerned about Welsh affairs, he wrote to the English press on key issues relating to the economic and political condition of Wales. In 1868, he stood as Liberal candidate in the constituency of Merthyr Tydfil and Aberdare, topping the poll. His election marked a turning-point in Welsh history. In Parliament, he spoke strongly in favour of Wales and of nonconformity, gaining himself the title of 'the Member for Wales'. (See DWB).

THOMAS, David Alfred (1856-1918), first Viscount Rhondda, was the son of Samuel Thomas who sank Ysguborwen pit in Aberdare. D. A. Thomas was born in Ysguborwen House. Educated at Clifton and Cambridge, he went to Clydach Vale to learn coal-mining first-hand. His real interest was politics, but after a disappointing political career, he turned his attention to establishing the Cambrian Combine which had a capital of £2,000,000. He returned to politics under Lloyd George's ministry and, in 1916, was made a peer, Baron Rhondda of Llanwern. He rendered great public service as Food Minister in 1917 when he devised a system of food rationing. (See DWB).

THOMAS, William (1794-1858), was a native of Merthyr Tydfil where his father was a maltster. He was trained as a doctor. He married Jane, daughter of Samuel Rees of the Werfa Estate in Aberdare who had acquired the Court Estate in Merthyr Tydfil from the Lewises of the Van. When Jane married William Thomas she took with her the Court Estate, an important asset. Bluff, genial and ambitious, William Thomas was an influential figure in parish affairs in Merthyr Tydfil. He was buried in St. John's churchyard, Aberdare, with his wife and son.

WAYNE, Matthew (c.1780-1853), was born in Somerset and came into prominence as a young man when he was appointed as furnace manager for Richard Crawshay at Cyfarthfa Ironworks. Crawshay left him £800 in his Will which Wayne invested in Nantyglo Ironworks where he became a partner of Joseph Bailey. His profits from this enterprise enabled him to set up a business of his own. In 1827, he established the Gadlys Ironworks at Aberdare which prospered and expanded despite its smallness in comparison with others in the area.

Matthew Wayne was a pioneer in the coal trade in the Aberdare valley; he sank the first pit for 'sale' coal at Abernantygroes, Cwmbach, in 1837. The production of 'steam coal' for sale was a novel venture for an ironmaster to embark upon and it was his good fortune that he struck the celebrated four-feet seam. His son, Thomas Wayne, is generally credited with having taken the initiative in this operation, but, collectively, Matthew Wayne and his sons brought to public notice the valuable properties of Aberdare steam coal. This led to spectacular developments in the coal industry in the valley. Matthew Wayne was a loyal and generous member of Hên Dy Cwrdd (the Unitarian meeting house), at Cefn Coed-y-Cymmer near Merthyr Tydfil, where he and his wife lie buried in the chapel graveyard. (See DWB).

WILLIAMS, David, 'Alaw Goch' (1809-1863), was a coal-owner and eisteddfodwr. In 1847, in partnership with Lewis Lewis, he sank Ynyscynon colliery in Cwmbach, Aberdare. From that venture, he went on to open a colliery at Aberaman and then sank Deep Duffryn pit at Mountain Ash which was later sold to John Nixon for £42,000. He used this money to sink another pit at Cwmdare in 1853 which he later sold at a profit. He bought land in Llanwonno, in the Rhondda valley and at Miskin Manor. He became a wealthy man but still maintained his contact with eisteddfodau and with the literary world in Wales. (See DWB).

Workers' houses in Plymouth Street, Merthyr Tydfil.

List of Primary Sources

1. *Manuscript Collections*

(a) Held in the Glamorgan Record Office:
(i) Merthyr Tydfil Union Minute Books, 1836-1876, 1879-1884, 1886-1891.
(ii) Merthyr Tydfil Union, Hospital Committee Minute Book, 1874-1881, including Industrial Training School Minutes and Reports, 1877-1883.
(iii) Merthyr Tydfil Union, Cholera Committee Minute Book, 1866.
(iv) Merthyr Tydfil Union, Abstracts of Accounts (printed), 1850-1894.
(v) Merthyr Tydfil Poor Rate, Letters concerning unrest, 1874-1875.
(vi) Glamorgan Quarter Sessions, Juvenile Convictions, Vol. 1.

(b) Held in the Public Record Office, London:
Poor Law Union Papers, Merthyr Tydfil Union, MH 12 Bundles 16326-16349 (1834-1894).

2. *Government publications*

(i) Report of the Royal Commission for Inquiring into the Administration and Practical Operation of the Laws for the Relief of the Poor, 21 February 1834.
(ii) The Report to the General Board of Health on a Preliminary Inquiry into the Sewerage, Drainage and Supply of Water and the Sanitary Condition of the Inhabitants of the Town of Merthyr Tydfil in the County of Glamorgan, by T. W. Rammell, Esq., 1850.
(iii) The Report to the General Board of Health, 1853, on a Preliminary Inquiry into the Sewerage, Drainage and Supply of Water and the Sanitary Condition of the Inhabitants of the Town of Aberdare in the County of Glamorgan, by T. W. Rammell, Esq., 1853.

3. *Newspapers*

(i) Held in Cardiff Central Library: *Cardiff and Merthyr Guardian*, 1834-1874.
(ii) Held in Glamorgan Record Office: *Merthyr Express*, 1864-1894.

Select Bibliography
(including works quoted)

Addis, J.P. (1957), *The Crawshay Dynasty*, University of Wales Press.

Anstruther, Ian (1984), *The Scandal of the Andover Workhouse*, Alan Sutton.

Bessborough, Earl of (1952), *The Diaries of Lady Charlotte Guest. Extracts from her Journal, 1833-1852*, John Murray.

Briggs, Asa (1968), *Victorian Cities*, Pelican Books.

Checkland, S. G. & E. O. A. (1984), *The Poor Law Report*, Pelican Books.

Chesney, K. (1990), *The Victorian Underworld*, Temple Smith.

Crowther, M.A. (1983), *The Workhouse System*, Methuen.

Cynon Valley History Society Publications, Vols. 1-6.

Davies, A.C. (1977), 'The Old Poor Law in an Industrializing Parish, Aberdare, 1818-1836', *The Welsh History Review*, Vol. 8, No. 3.

Dickens, Charles (1838), *Oliver Twist*.

Digby, A. (1978), *Pauper Palaces*.

Digby, A. (1982), *The Poor Law in Nineteenth-Century England and Wales*.

Evans, D. G. (1989), *A History of Wales 1815-1906*, University of Wales Press.

Finer, S. E. (1952), *The Life and Times of Sir Edwin Chadwick*, Methuen.

Fraser, D. (1976), *The New Poor Law in the Nineteenth Century*.

Fraser, D. (1984), *The Evolution of the British Welfare State*.

Ginswick, Jules (ed.) (1983), *Labour and the Poor in England and Wales 1849-1851*, Vol. III, Frank Cass.

Grant, R. K. J. (1988), *On the Parish*, Glamorgan Archive Service, Cardiff.

Grant, R. K. J. (1991) *Cynon Valley in the Age of Iron*, Cynon Valley Borough Council.

Gregg, Pauline (1956), *A Social and Economic History of Britain 1760-1955*, Harrap.

Hayman, Richard (1989), *Working Iron in Merthyr Tydfil*, Merthyr Tydfil Heritage Trust.

Henriques, Ursula (1979), *Before the Welfare State*, Longman.

Hill, C. P. (1972), *British Economic and Social History 1700-1964*, Arnold.

John, A. H. (1950), *The Industrial Development of South Wales*, University of Wales Press.

Jones, Ieuan Gwynedd (1987), *Communities*, Gomer Press.

Littlewood, Kevin (1990), *From Reform to Charter*, Merthyr Tydfil Heritage Trust.

Longmate, Norman (1974), *The Workhouse*, Temple Smith.

Lowe, J. B. (1977), *Welsh Industrial Workers Housing 1775-1875*, National Museum of Wales.

Merthyr Teachers' Centre Group (1981), *Merthyr Tydfil. A Valley Community*, Merthyr Teachers' Centre Group.

Merthyr Tydfil Historical Society, *Merthyr Historian*, Vols. 1-4.

Moore, Donald (1988), *Artists' Views of Glamorgan: the Nineteenth Century*, Glamorgan Archive Service, Cardiff.

Morris, J. H., and Williams, L. J. (1958), *The South Wales Coal Industry 1841-1875*, University of Wales Press.

Owen, John A. (1977), *The History of the Dowlais Works 1759-1970*, Starling Press.

Parry, R. I. (1984), 'Early Industrial Relations in Aberdare', *Old Aberdare*, Vol. 3, Cynon Valley History Society.

Pike, E. Royston (1974), *Human Documents of the Victorian Golden Age*, Allen & Unwin.

Rose, Michael E. (1971), *The English Poor Law 1780-1930*, David & Charles.

Stedman Jones, Gareth (1971), *Outcast London*, Penguin Books.

Strange, Keith (undated), *Merthyr Tydfil in the 1840s*, Mid Glamorgan Education Department (History Research Group).

Treble, J. H. (1979), *Urban Poverty in Britain, 1830-1914*.

Webb, Sidney and Beatrice (1963 reprint), *English Poor Law Policy*, Frank Cass.

Wiliam, Eurwyn (1987), Rhydycar—A Welsh Mining Community, National Museum of Wales.

Williams, D. (1982), *A History of Modern Wales*, John Murrary.

Williams, Glanmor (ed.) (1966), *Merthyr Politics: The Making of a Working-Class Tradition*, University of Wales Press.

Williams, Gwyn A. (1978), *The Merthyr Rising*, Croom Helm.

Williams, Gwyn A. (1985), *When was Wales?*, Penguin Books.

Wohl, A. S. (1983), *Endangered Lives*, Dent.

Wood, Peter (1991), *Poverty and the Workhouse in Victorian Britain*, Alan Sutton.

Acknowledgements—Illustrations

All illustrations, with the exception of those listed below, come from collections within the Glamorgan Record Office. The author and the publishers wish to express their thanks to the following individuals, institutions and organisations for permission, in every case readily granted, to reproduce items from their collections:

Aberdare Masonic Temple: p. 47
British Library, London: pp.86, 87, 161
Cyfarthfa Castle Museum and Art Gallery: pp. 2, 73
Cynon Valley Libraries: pp. 27, 60, 120, 123 *(above)*
Guildhall Library, City of London: p. 138
Gwynedd Archives: p. 119
Jeremy Lowe: pp. 48, 174
The Hulton Deutsch Collection: pp. 6, 34, 89, 100
Mary Evans Picture Library: p. 55
Merthyr Tydfil Public Libraries: pp. 25, 125, 134
R. D. Whitaker: p. 3
The Royal Photographic Society, Bath: p. 63
University College London: p. 15
Welsh Industrial and Maritime Museum: pp. 16, 130, 131
York City Art Gallery: p. 91

Thanks are due to Mid Glamorgan Education Department for permission to base the map on p. 42 on one by Clive Thomas published in *Merthyr Tydfil in the 1840's*, by Keith Strange; also to the Welsh Office, to the University of Wales Press, and to Croom Helm, for permission to reproduce the map on page xiv, published in *People, Protest and Politics*, by David Egan.

Permission has been received, and is gratefully acknowledged, from Alan Sutton to quote from *The Scandal of the Andover Workhouse*, by Ian Anstruther; also from Frank Cass to quote from *Labour and the Poor in England and Wales 1849-1851, Letters to* The Morning Chronicle, edited by Jules Ginswick.

May 9602 The Committee were attended by the Medical
Gentleman of the parish of Merthyr and by several of the
principal Inhabitants

9603 Mr Job James the Medical Officer of the Union
certified that Asiatic Cholera had reached the District
and that several deaths had ensued

9604 Mr Wrenn Sup't of Police was requested and
undertook to superintend the distributing of lime all
over the town of Merthyr and white liming where
necessary and the clerk was directed to give orders
for any materials required and that paupers be placed
under Mr Wrenn's directions.

9605 The Clerk was directed to print and distribute
the following

Notice

The Asiatic Cholera having beyond doubt appeared in
Merthyr and proved fatal in many cases especially in
the dirtier parts of the Town the Inhabitants are earnestly
requested to pay the greatest attention to the Cleanliness of
their Houses more particularly by White Washing them
inside and outside and by not allowing any dirty or
offensive matter to collect near their Houses.

The outbreak of Asiatic Cholera in the district,
29 May 1849.

179

SELECTIVE INDEX

Figures in **bold** refer to illustrations

H

,